Another

30 New Zealand Stories for Children

Another 30 New Zealand Stories for Children

Edited by Barbara Else
Illustrations by David Elliot

RANDOM HOUSE
NEW ZEALAND

For Rosa and Olive who love a good story
and for Abe who liked stories even before he was born—B.E.

To the memory of Kelly, the dog who inspired many
of the animal drawings in these books—D.E.

National Library of New Zealand Cataloguing-in-Publication Data

Another 30 New Zealand stories for children / edited by Barbara Else;
illustrations by David Elliot.
Sequel to: 30 New Zealand stories for children.
Includes index.
ISBN 1-86941-535-3
1. Children's stories, New Zealand. 2. Short stories, New Zealand.
I. Else, Barbara. II. Elliot, David, 1952-
NZ823.01089282—dc 21

A RANDOM HOUSE BOOK
published by
Random House New Zealand
18 Poland Road, Glenfield, Auckland, New Zealand
www.randomhouse.co.nz

First published 2002

ISBN 1 86941 535 3

Cover image inspired by 'Uncle Trev, Old Tip and Old Toot' written by Jack Lasenby
Cover illustration: David Elliot
Printed in Hong Kong

Contents

Acknowledgements

The publishers gratefully acknowledge the following authors and publishers for permission to reproduce the stories. Where there is no publishing credit, the story is previously unpublished and all rights remain with the authors.

'People in Glasshouses', © Bronwyn Bannister.
'The Earth Moving Business', © Fleur Beale.
'Three Plump Pigeons', © Margaret Beames, first published by Nelson Price Milburn Ltd, Auckland, 1990.
'The Whispering Mat', © Kath Beattie.
'Mars Bar', © Norman Bilbrough, first published in *School Journal,* part 1, No. 2, 1997, by Learning Media Ltd, for the Ministry of Education.
'Foxy', © Jane Buxton, first published in *School Journal,* part 2, No. 3, 1991, by Learning Media Ltd, for the Ministry of Education.
'Cliff Minestrone', © Kate De Goldi.
'The Opposite Weather Boy', © Chris Else.
'Sky', © Peter Friend, first published in *School Journal,* part 1, No. 1, 1999, by Learning Media Ltd, for the Ministry of Education.
'Āreta and the Kahawai', © Patricia Grace, originally published in 1994, under the Puffin imprint, and reproduced with permission by Penguin Books (NZ) Ltd.
'How Hugo Wart Hog Found True Happiness', © Roger Hall.
'Wonder Waffles', © Huberta Hellendoorn.
'The Giant with Eyes on Her Knees', © Barbara Hill.
'Takes Two', © David Hill.
'The Moon', © Adrienne Jansen, first broadcast by Radio New Zealand.
'Uncle Trev, Old Tip and Old Toot', © Jack Lasenby, *Uncle Trev,* Cape Catley, 1991.
'Uncle Barney's Buttons', © Janice Leitch.
'Going for Gold', © Sandy McKay.
'Mere: Ghost Investigator', © C. Todd Maguire. The author would like to acknowledge her family and Room 10, 1996, Te Huruhi Primary School, Waiheke Island.
'Class Photo', Janice Marriott; reproduced by permission of the publishers Learning Media Ltd, for the Ministry of Education, © Learning Media Ltd, 2002.
'What the Wind Does', © Janice Marriott.
'Hazel and the Neanderthal', © Jennifer Maxwell.
'A Hāngi After All', © Barbara Murison, first published in *Jabberwocky,* Vol. 8, No. 4, February 1993.
'The Dance Hall Ghost', © Diana Noonan, first published in *School Journal,* part 3, No. 1, 2001, by Learning Media Ltd, for the Ministry of Education.
'Dirty Dishes', © Gillian Price, first published in *School Journal,* part 3, No. 3, 2001, by Learning Media Ltd, for the Ministry of Education.
'Grandpa's Gooseberry Bush', © Elizabeth Pulford.
'William's Words', © Pat Quinn, first published in *Blast Off!* No. 7, Vol. 73, 1988 (NSW Dept. Education).
'The Plum Tree', © Paora Tibble, first published in *School Journal,* part 2, No. 1, 2002, by Learning Media Ltd, for the Ministry of Education.
'The Day I Wore a Dress', © Penelope Todd.
'Wet', © Jane Westaway.

1

The Day I Wore a Dress

Penelope Todd

Four ladies twittered around me. Flowers sprouted from every inch of me. Mrs Hector was on her knees, pinning the fifty-third hydrangea to my chest. It covered the last patch of pink dress.

"There," she said, straightening. "A real princess. Which is a marvel, considering that boyish little figure." Mrs Helps tut-tutted over my 'short back and sides' as she adjusted the thirty-seven-rosebud-hairband that felt like a wild cat riding my head. How on earth had Tess talked me into this? I'd get her later, spots or no spots.

My sister had got chicken-pox the day before she was to be princess on the Plucky Poultry Festival Float. Propped in bed, Tess had clutched my arm and hissed, "You'll do it for me, Tom. No one'll know you're not me. Plus, with make-up you won't even look like *you*."

"You've got to be kidding," I said. Yes, she's my twin

9

and yes, since Tess's haircut we do get mistaken for each other. But, me a princess? No way.

Tess's grip tightened. Hard to believe she was sick except for the ugly red blotches on her face. "You'll do it, Tom. The bike race. Remember?"

My heart sank.

When I'd sprained my ankle two months ago, I'd begged and pleaded and made crazy promises to Tess if only she'd enter the last BMX race of the year in my name. So I'd at least have a chance of making the Mud Fish squad next season.

And she'd done it. Dragged up every bit of guts and jumped on my bike at the top of Suicide Circuit. Helmet on, padded to the max, she could've been me, the way she threw the bike into the jumps, the swerves, the mud holes. And won the race.

"Remember?" Tess's fingers twisted. "You said *anything* I asked before we're thirteen. Buddy, this is it. You are Tess McFerrin, Poultry Princess, 2002. And if you win Festival Queen, we'll split that ten kilograms of chocolate."

She sank back on the pillows and whispered, "Go and tell Mum."

"Well," said Mum, "I suppose you might get away with it. You only have to smile and wave."

"What if they ask questions?" I said.

Tess shrieked from the bedroom, "You don't need a *personality* or I wouldn't be asking you."

Next morning, right after soccer, when she'd zipped me into Tess's long pink dress that was so tight I couldn't even sigh, Mum gave me the pink shoes in a bag. Too small by centimetres.

"Put them on at the last minute," she said. "And have a gorgeous time." She winked. And giggled, as Dad tooted the car horn.

"Yeah, thanks," I muttered, running onto the porch. Where were my shoes? Dad tooted again. I grabbed my soccer boots, shoved my feet in, galloped to the car.

Too late for regrets now. The ladies hoisted me onto the float without bashing off any blooms.

"Stand on the big green circle, Tess, dear," Mrs Helps was saying. "It rotates slowly so all you have to do is wave."

"And smile, smile, smile," said Mrs Hector.

I felt like a doll in a music box. But I managed a crazed smile that got a bit hysterical when I remembered the red lipstick and blue eye-shadow they'd plastered on me. I waved like the woman on the purple Maindrag Meats float behind us.

The crowd waved back and clapped. There was the odd wolf-whistle. I grinned as I rotated slowly to the music. This was easy.

Until we stopped.

Oh no! Half my soccer team was on the footpath. There was Ben Scott, big fan of Tess. Craning his neck for a good gawk. I shuffled against the slow spin of the platform, trying to get my back to him.

Then the loud-speaker called for attention and all the floats formed a frozen semi-circle. The music shut off but something scary was happening under me. My platform was speeding up. My feet were skipping and tripping over each other. I tried jumping but each time I landed the

11

spinning disc tossed me off balance and I'd have to leap again. People tittered. Then they laughed. Ben frowned, then he folded in the middle. Cracking up. He screamed and slapped the others.

"Hold on, Tess!" called Mrs Hector from the front of the float. "We're getting help."

Now the platform was rising under me, a metre above the truck bed, still revolving. My feet drummed as the dress ballooned up. I spread my arms for balance over the whirling tutu of hydrangeas, flinging off one by one into the audience. I clenched my fists and danced faster as the air rushed under the dress.

I couldn't fall in front of this crowd.

"That's it!" someone shouted. There was a clunk, a whining. The platform sank and juddered to a stop.

I lurched upright, trying to look dignified, fixing my eyes far over the heads of this juvenile crowd.

The judge tried to speak but each time he raised the megaphone he exploded, "Pshaw, haw, haw!"

Ben was staring at me, open-mouthed. He nudged Josh Thomas and pointed. I looked down. The dress had flicked up on itself. I peered over.

Dirty knees, blue soccer socks, muddy boots.

"And the novelty prize," the judge was still giggling, "goes to the Plucky Poultry Princess for sheer pluck and fancy footwear . . . I mean, footwork. The prize? Twenty litres of Barbie-Belle Bubble Bath. That should clean up those knees, eh folks?"

I saw my mates taking in the information. I looked at the barrel of pink glug the judge was dumping at my feet.

I looked at the road and I hit it, running.

I was hurrying home to my dear sister. I had a dress for her, flowers, some choice words and a special twenty-litre treat for her bath tonight.

Spots or no spots.

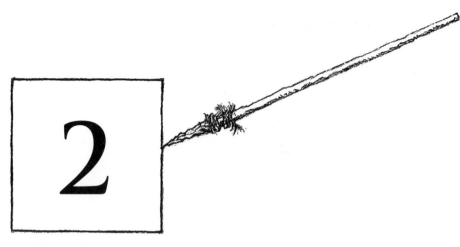

2

Hazel and the Neanderthal

Jennifer Maxwell

"Don't look now, Nanna Belle," said Hazel, "but there's a Neanderthal at the window."

"Dear me," said Nanna Belle. "I hope not. I don't like surprises."

"It's only a *little* Neanderthal," said Hazel. "The one we saw at the museum yesterday. I think he must be lonely."

"We're getting too old for surprises," said Nanna Belle. "Aren't we, Harry?"

Harry looked at Hazel's toast and licked his whiskery lips.

"I was only trying to warn you," said Hazel sadly to the dog.

Nanna Belle turned to the kitchen sink, pulled on her rubber gloves with a *snap*, lifted her head and looked out the window. And out of the morning darkness, a face looked back at her. A very dirty face with small black eyes, big black eyebrows and a great deal of spiky black hair.

"Arggh!" it said, and disappeared.

"Ohhh!" said Nanna Belle and sank very softly, very gently, down the kitchen cupboards to the floor.

"Oh dear," said Hazel, and gave her toast to Harry.

She placed a cushion under Nanna Belle's head and spread the damp dishcloth on her brow. Then she opened the door. The lavender bushes trembled. "Out you come," she said. "I know you're there."

A grubby finger parted the bushes. A nose appeared. Two frightened eyes.

"Poor thing," said Hazel. "You were brave to come here, all on your own. Don't be scared. I won't hurt you."

And the creature poked its head out of the lavender, looked left and right and hurled itself into Hazel's open arms.

"Poof!" said Hazel. "You smell awful. I expect that's normal for a Neanderthal. But you can't walk round town dressed like that. You better come inside."

The Neanderthal saw Nanna Belle lying on the floor with her eyes shut and did a triumphant war dance, waving his wooden spear and shaking his sharp stone axe.

"Stop that!" said Hazel. "Nanna Belle doesn't want any more surprises—and leave poor Harry alone!" The Neanderthal had spotted Harry and they were nose to nose under the table, growling ferociously.

"Be quiet!" said Hazel. "Sit down, Harry!"

Harry sat. The Neanderthal stopped growling. Hazel grabbed his hand and pulled him into Nanna Belle's spare bedroom.

"Hmm," said Hazel, looking at his big, bushy bearskin. "Just a T-shirt, I think." But getting a T-shirt onto a Neanderthal was very, very difficult, especially when the Neanderthal was ambushing a teddy bear in the middle of the bed.

"Here," said Hazel. "Look at this, instead." She opened her favourite picture book and propped it against the bear.

Sabre-toothed tigers. A herd of woolly mammoths.

The Neanderthal's jaw dropped. So did his axe and spear. He stood perfectly still, staring at the pages while Hazel dressed him in her daffodil T-shirt and her biggest, floppiest hat.

He still looked rather odd. Like a very short woman with big hairy knickers and huge dirty feet.

"I'm sure no one will notice," said Hazel. "Now, what's your name?"

The Neanderthal stared at her. Hazel pointed to herself. "Hazel," she said. Then she pointed at him.

"Hob," said the Neanderthal.

"Hob," said Hazel, and smiled.

"We're going to play in the park," said Hazel to Nanna Belle. "Do you want to come?"

Nanna Belle opened one eye and looked at Hob. Harry growled from under the table. "I think I'll stay here," said Nanna Belle, "and have a little rest."

Hob tore up Nanna Belle's carnations and stuffed them into his mouth.

"Poor Hob," said Hazel. "I expect you missed your

breakfast." She took him to the corner store and bought him green jelly babies with her holiday money.

Hob stared at the jelly babies, perplexed. He stood one on his hand and made horrible faces at it.

"Like this," said Hazel and bit off a jelly baby head.

Hob's eyes opened wide. Very, very cautiously, he nibbled a jelly baby foot.

"Ummm!" he said and crammed them, paper bag and all, into his mouth.

"Peculiar little fellow," said the shopkeeper with a frown.

The traffic roared at the lights. Hob roared back. Hazel pressed the button to cross the road and the little green man appeared.

"Ummm!" said Hob and hurled his spear at it.

"Hooligan!" shouted a bus driver. Hazel dragged Hob across.

Hob chased the dogs in the park until their owners chased him back. He jumped into the goldfish pond and made wet clay handprints all along the path.

"Behave yourself!" said a man in a suit, and poked Hob in the bearskin with his umbrella. Hob climbed a tree and howled at him and pelted him with nuts. The man complained to the dog owners. The dog owners complained to the park gardeners. The gardeners saw the handprints on the paths and shook their rakes and roared.

"Hob," said Hazel as they hid in the bushes. "This won't do. You'll have to go home to your mum and dad." She pointed to the museum on the other side of the park. "I expect they're missing you."

Hob looked sad which made Hazel sad as well. "I expect *my* mother and father are missing me too," she said and a tear ran down her nose.

Hob put his dirty brown hands on hers.

Deep within the museum, a fire glowed at the opening to a cave. Beside the fire, a little brown baby yawned in a pile of furs. Hob's mother was making a meal of berries and leaves. She smiled gently at Hazel just before she froze into position for the day. Hob's father raised his spear and shielded his eyes from the morning sun and as he did, he winked at her, just like her own father did. Hob scrambled to his lookout above the cave and sat very still, his eyes fixed on Hazel's. Beneath the wall of glass that closed them in, a sign read:

A Family of Neanderthals

"That's better," said Hazel. "I'll visit *you* from now on. Every day, until I go home to my mum and dad."

Dirty Dishes

Gillian Findsen

"Pete!" called Dad. "Load the dishwasher, will ya? And turn it on."

Peter looked up from the trading cards he was sorting. Perhaps he'd just pretend he hadn't heard.

"Pete?" Dad's head appeared at the door to Peter's bedroom. "I can see that you're doing something really important," he said in his best sarcastic voice, "but Mum won't be back till late, and it won't hurt you to do the dishes."

"It might," muttered Peter when Dad had gone again.

Peter would never say it out loud to anyone, but the new dishwasher was really creepy. It was never a problem for anyone else, but it always played up when HE tried to use it. Lately, he'd had the weirdest feeling that the dishwasher was just waiting to get him.

The kitchen was dark when he went into it. The first thing he did was flick on all the lights—even the ones over the stove. The dinner dishes were piled on the bench. There seemed to be an awful lot of them for just four people.

He eyed the dishwasher cautiously. Knives and forks seemed to go missing after they'd been loaded into that machine. His camping set had never appeared again, and his favourite glasses and cups always came out chipped or broken.

Slowly he reached out to the dishwasher door and pulled it open. Instantly there was a gurgling rumble, a cough and the water that sat in the bottom of the thing spat out at him. Peter jumped back.

He COULD wash all the dishes by hand, but it would take a long, long time. Dad would want to know why he wasn't using the machine, and he didn't want to have to explain. It would sound so stupid.

Gingerly, Peter placed a glass in the top rack of the dishwasher. So far so good. He put the rest of the glasses in, then the cups.

"Come on, now," he encouraged as he slid the bottom rack out.

It was no good. The minute he put the first plate in the rack, the machine gave a hiccup and a moan. Peter swung round, hoping that the noise had come from someone behind him. It hadn't. He was alone in the kitchen.

At the second plate, the water in the bottom of the dishwasher began to swirl.

"Not many more," Peter lied, lifting in the third plate. His coaxing was greeted with a sigh, and then a thin, watery voice gurgled, "Too much."

Peter looked around again. He wouldn't put it past his sister, Clare, to sneak up on him and put on a spooky voice like that.

She wasn't there.

Quickly he began almost throwing the dirty dishes into the racks. Plates, bowls, pots, and pans went in any old how.

The watery voice got louder and louder. "Too much, too much, TOO MUCH!"

"Stop it!" hissed Peter as loud as he dared.

He loaded in the last plastic bowl and reached for the detergent.

Without any warning, a bowl suddenly flew out and onto the floor. The cutlery basket was right behind it. Knives, forks, and spoons seemed to be coming right for him. Peter dived behind a chair and covered his head with his arms. As the last spoon hit his hand, he heard footsteps.

"What on earth are you doing, Peter?" said Dad.

"Sorry," said Peter. "I dropped the knives and forks."

"Get on with the job," was Dad's reply.

"What's WRONG with you?" demanded Peter when Dad had gone out again. He looked around at the dirty cutlery spread over the kitchen floor. There were traces of Marmite on the lino, and there was a smear of butter across one of the cupboard doors. Suddenly he felt really mad.

"You don't do this with anyone else!" he told the dishwasher. At the same time, he recognised Mum's don't-mess-around-with-me tone in his own voice. "Stop this behaviour at once!" he said.

The dishwasher gave a little cough and then a gurgle.

For the first time, Peter felt as if he was getting somewhere with it. He crossed his arms over his chest, just like Mum did when she was telling him off for something.

"I'm sick of this!" he told the dishwasher. "I've got to load these dishes, and you've got to wash them whether you like it or not."

As he spoke, he reloaded the plastic bowl firmly into the rack. He gathered the cutlery, slammed it into its basket, and thumped the basket into place. He wiped up the butter and Marmite without once turning his back on the dishwasher. Finally, he filled the detergent dispenser, clicked its lid shut, and slammed the dishwasher door.

A very small gurgle could be heard, and then there was silence.

Peter pushed the buttons on the dishwasher's control panel. He set the machine onto its longest, strongest cycle.

"Now, get to work!" he instructed. "And let this be a lesson to you!"

"Something wrong, Pete?" asked Dad.

"Huh?"

Dad was leaning against the doorway, looking at him strangely.

"No," replied Peter firmly as he flicked off the last of the kitchen lights. "You just have to know how to treat that dishwasher properly."

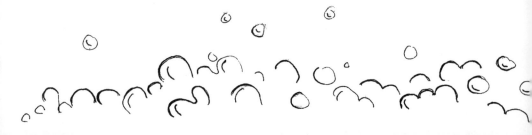

Grandpa's Gooseberry Bush

Elizabeth Pulford

Every summer when the sun shone bright and the gooseberries were hanging yellow and ripe Jessica went to stay with Grandpa and Grandma.

And on the sunniest day Jessica and Grandpa walked to the whiskery gooseberry bush tucked behind the tumbling-down shed at the bottom of the garden.

Jessica always carried a red pail and Grandpa a blue one.

Together they picked the gooseberries and when the pails were full they trailed back up to the house where Grandpa placed the pails on the kitchen bench.

To which Grandma would exclaim, "Oh my!" And rattle around her cupboards for pie dishes.

Then, as always, Jessica and Grandpa would help Grandma bake the gooseberry pies.

And in the early evening when the wind had dropped and white moths fluttered around the long grass the three of them would sit on the back wooden steps and eat one of the pies. And there they would stay until the moon came up and made spooky shadows and if they were lucky they would hear an owl hooting in the old oak tree.

After a bit Grandpa would say, "That was the best pie yet. What do you say, Jessica?"

To which, Jessica would reply, "The best one ever."

While Grandma nodded.

Then one summer when Jessica and Grandpa went down to the bottom of the garden, carrying their pails as usual, and rounded the corner of the shed, they both stopped in horror.

For there, looking as bristly and gristly as ever, sat the grand gooseberry bush but with hardly a gooseberry.

"Oh dear," said Grandpa, bending over and lifting up one of its lichen limbs.

"Is it sick?" asked Jessica.

Grandpa shook his head and sighed. "It's getting old. But there should be enough for one pie."

So Jessica and Grandpa carefully picked off every last gooseberry. Then before they went up to the house, Grandpa said, "Not just yet. We have work to do."

And so with Grandpa leading the way, the two of them went into the tumbling-down shed. "Now," he said, looking around the crowded shelves. "Where are they?" Then, "Ah yes, here we are." He picked up a pair of snips.

"What are they for?" asked Jessica.

"You'll see."

After which the two of them left the tumbling-down shed and went back to the gooseberry bush. Kneeling down Grandpa snipped off a branch then, handing the snips to Jessica, said, "Your turn."

Jessica chose a thick thorny branch and minding the prickles she clipped it off.

"Now we need to trim them." And as he stripped the leaves Jessica did the same.

"Right, they're ready for planting." And so saying Grandpa pushed his cutting into the dirt beside the old gooseberry bush. Jessica planted her twig on the other side.

"Now we'll have to wait and see," smiled Grandpa and touched the side of his nose, like he did when he knew a secret.

The following summer the sky wasn't as blue as usual and the sun didn't shine as much and Grandpa had a cough. And when the two of them went down to the bottom of the garden, Jessica saw that there were no leaves on Grandpa's old gooseberry bush and its prickles were white with age. And she knew it had died.

"I'm sorry, Grandpa."

"Nothing lives forever, Jessica. Not even a gruff old gooseberry bush. Oh, you can be sad for a while but then you've just got to get on with things. Everything is replaced in its own time." And he pointed to the two cuttings they had planted last year, both now bustling with bright green leaves.

"There are no gooseberries," said Jessica.

"Not this year. But wait until next."

So that night they didn't have gooseberry pie and Grandpa didn't say, "That was the best pie yet." And Jessica didn't reply, "The best ever." And Grandma didn't nod. Nor did the moon shine. Instead it rained. So they stayed inside and ate apple crumble and traced the raindrops trickling down the window with their fingers.

That winter Grandpa died.

In the summer when Jessica went to stay with Grandma there was an aching space of silence. No more the sound of Grandpa's soft footsteps or his gentle whistle. No more his throaty chuckle or his warm voice, instead a solemn stillness. So Jessica tiptoed everywhere trying not to disturb this new sound.

On the hottest day she helped Grandma tidy the house. Then she made a hut in the bush. But it was no good. She knew what she had to do, even though it might upset Grandma.

Going inside, Jessica picked up Grandpa's blue pail and her red one. Then she headed towards the tumbling-down shed and kneeling down between the two new gooseberry bushes she began to pick the gooseberries. First plopping the ones from Grandpa's bush into his blue pail. Then plopping those from her bush into the red pail. And when she had finished she walked back up to the house and standing on tiptoes placed the two pails on the kitchen bench.

Grandma looked at them, her eyes shimmering with tears. "Oh my," she whispered and rummaged around the cupboards for two pie dishes.

That evening Jessica and Grandma sat on the wooden steps at the back of the house and ate the pie made from Grandpa's new gooseberry bush. And there they stayed until the moon came up and made spooky shadows and the owl hooted in the old oak tree.

And in her mind Jessica heard Grandpa say, "That was the best pie yet. What do you say, Jessica?"

To which she silently replied, "The best one ever."

And when Jessica looked over at Grandma she knew she had done the right thing. For there she was nodding and smiling quietly to herself.

The Earth Moving Business

Fleur Beale

I'm in the earth moving business. I've got trucks with trailers and trucks that tip. I've got diggers and bulldozers. I've got dump trucks and loaders. But I've got a bit of a problem. I don't have much earth to move.

On Saturday morning I got out my digger. I drove it around the side of our house and into the driveway. Wow! There was a big pile of dirt. It was in the middle of Mrs Mannaby's driveway.

I had a funny feeling about that big pile of dirt. I felt that Mrs Mannaby might not want it in the middle of her driveway.

I had to hurry. I ran and banged on Mike's door. "Bring your machines. We've got dirt at Mrs Mannaby's."

In next to no time, Mike and I were bulldozing roads. We were digging. We were dumping. We were trucking loads from one side of the big pile of dirt to the other.

Then Mrs Mannaby came out. I was right. She didn't

want dirt in her driveway. "That useless tip truck driver!" she yelled. "I told him to tip it in the garden!"

She said to Mike and me, "Does this driveway look like a garden to you?"

"No," Mike said.

"Not at all," I said.

She got out her phone and rang the driver.

She talked on the phone and kicked the dirt. She said, "I want the dirt in my garden. I don't want it in my driveway." She stopped and listened. Then she yelled, "But you have to come and fix it! It's going to rain! There'll be a terrible mess."

She got off the phone and said to Mike and me, "He's not coming." Wow! We could play in the dirt forever. But then she said, "What'll I do? I can't move all this dirt before the rain starts. If it gets wet there'll be mud, mud and more mud."

That sounded good to me and Mike. But we could tell she was upset. "We'll move it for you," I said. After all, we were in the earth moving business.

It was a big offer. But she went on being upset. "You won't be able to do it before the rain starts."

"We'll get help," I said. We ran down the road.

"Come and help move Mrs Mannaby's dirt pile," I told Cassie.

"Come and help move Mrs Mannaby's dirt pile," Mike told Jason.

"No," said Jason.

"Cassie's coming," I said. Jason went and got a shovel and a wheelbarrow. Mum came to help. Dad came to help. Two people from down the road came to help.

Mrs Mannaby smiled again. "We might get it done before the rain comes," she said.

Mike and I hitched our machines together. We hitched the tip truck to the articulated truck. Then we hitched on the trailer. Then we hitched the dump truck to the trailer.

We filled up each truck. We used the digger and the bulldozer. People kept getting in our way.

"Watch out, you two," said Dad.

"Out of my way," said Jason.

Well! It was our idea in the first place.

"We have to change our equipment," I said to Mike. "We have to move with the times."

"Like how?" he asked. He doesn't always have too many ideas.

"Get your skateboard," I said. I got mine. I got rope. I got the washing basket. I put a big plastic bag inside it. I tied it onto the two skateboards. I made a handle.

"Cool!" said Mike. "It's a basket cart."

"No," I said. "It's an earth transporter." See what I mean about Mike? He doesn't always have too many ideas.

The dirt pile was getting smaller. We filled our earth transporter with dirt. We pulled it down the drive. We tipped the dirt onto the garden.

Jason tipped his wheelbarrow full of dirt out beside us. He laughed at our earth transporter. Cassie came with her bucket full of dirt. "What a great invention!" she said. "I wish I'd thought of that." She gave me a hug.

Jason looked sick.

Mrs Mannaby said, "Wonderful! Wonderful! We might get done before the rain comes."

Dad said, "My son the inventor!" He patted my head.

Mum said, "I hope you wash that basket when you've finished with it." Sometimes my mother just can't see the big picture.

We worked. We dug the dirt. We filled the earth transporter. We pulled it. We tipped it. We got tired but we kept going.

The sky got darker. Some fat drops of rain fell. The dirt pile got smaller. The sky got darker still. We dug faster. We ran faster. We tipped faster. The sky got darker still. The dirt pile got smaller. Our shovels scraped on the driveway. More fat drops of rain fell.

"We've nearly finished," said Mrs Mannaby.

Mike and I tipped our last load. The rain came down. It fell hard and fast.

"That's okay," said Mrs Mannaby. "It'll wash the driveway clean." She gave us hot drinks and apple cake.

Mike and I took our machinery home. "I wish we had a dirt pile of our own," I said.

The next fine day, Mrs Mannaby knocked on our door. "Come with me," she said.

She walked to the garden behind her house. "See that corner?" she said.

I saw it. It had good dirt in it. It would be the best place to use my earth moving machinery. "That's for you and Mike," she said. "I don't need all this garden. I don't need all this dirt." She patted my head.

I gave her a huge hug. Then I ran and banged on Mike's door. "Bring your machines. We've got dirt at Mrs Mannaby's!"

The Giant with Eyes on Her Knees

Barbara Hill

The Giant was so tall, she had an extra pair of eyes on her knees, so she could see where her feet were going.

When she went out walking, her Knee-cap Eyes would guide her.

"Look out. There's a house coming up," they would warn, and the Giant would step sideways, because she was a kindly giant, and she didn't like scrunching things.

When people saw her coming, they stood very still, and knew they would be safe. With her Knee-cap Eyes on the watch, the Giant was no danger at all.

Summer came, and the Giant was hot.

She sat on the mountain top, where the breezes blow, but still she was hot.

"I'll try the sea," she decided. "I'll go and paddle."

So she went to the beach, took off her shoes and socks, and waded into the water.

"Ahh! That's cool. That's cooool," she sighed.

But her Knee-cap Eyes cried out, "No! No! this water is too salty. It stings! It stings! Ooooh!" and they clamped their eyelids tight shut, and wouldn't open them again.

The Giant didn't know where her feet were going. When she stepped back on the land, she flattened the Surf Club building. Lucky no one was in it . . .

Her second step scrunched the pigsty on Farmer Scrubbit's farm. Pigs squealed, hens flapped, and dogs scrambled out of the way. Farmer Scrubbit grabbed a pitch-fork, and jabbed it in the Giant's toe. The Giant stopped.

"What's going on down there?" she roared.

"Can't see. Can't see," cried the Knee-cap Eyes.

"We sting. We hurt. Can't see at all!" and they screwed themselves up tighter than before.

"Somebody do something," rumbled the Giant. "If I move, I'll squash some more."

"Stop! Wait! Stay there," yelled Farmer Scrubbit. "Don't move. I've got an idea." And he rushed inside and rang the fire brigade.

Soon, with a flurry of flashing lights, and wailing sirens, the fire engine arrived.

The firemen ran out their ladders and hoses, and squirted streams of fresh water onto the Knee-cap Eyes.

"Ah. That's better," they blinked. "We can see. We can see. Now Giant, we can tell you where to move."

But the Giant was not listening. She was bending over looking at the fire engine. She had never seen it working before.

"This is a handy wee thing," she murmured. "I'll keep it. If I wade in the water again tomorrow, I can wash my eyes out afterwards."

"No! No!" screamed the firemen, jumping up and down, and waving their hands in the air.

"No! No! That's our fire engine. You can't have that. We need it."

"What for?" boomed the Giant.

"For fires!" yelled the firemen. "A house might burn down. We need the fire engine to put out fires."

"Well," grumbled the Giant. "You think of another way to wash the salt out of my eyes, and I'll give it back to you. Until then, I'll keep it."

And she stamped away, back to the mountain top.

The people of the town held a meeting. "What shall we do? What shall we do? How can we get our fire engine back?" they asked.

There was silence while everybody thought hard, but no one had any ideas until Little Billy Crabtree said, "My eyes sting in the sea, so I wear goggles."

"Goggles!" shouted the Mayor. "We'll make the Giant some goggles."

Billy Crabtree giggled. "Goggles are no good on knees," he said. "They'd hold her knees together, and the Giant would fall over. You'll have to make her two separate Goggs."

"Well then, Goggs!" snapped the Mayor. "Who knows how to make Goggs?"

Nobody knew, so the bosses of all the big factories sat round a table, and invented some plans.

"Aluminium frames," said the man from the aluminium factory. "They'll be light and easy to wear. I can make those."

"Magnifying glass," said the man from the glass factory. "So she will see us better. I can make those."

"Rubber round the edges, so the water won't get in," said the man from the tyre factory. "I can make those."

"Straps and buckles to hold them in place," said the man from the leather factory. "I can make those."

They rushed away to their work places, where the lights blazed all night, and the machinery clanked and groaned, as they churned out their part of the Goggs.

In the morning, the Goggs were put together, and dragged to the beach.

When the Giant arrived for her paddle, the people were waiting. As she sat down to take off her shoes and socks, they swarmed all over her like ants.

"What's this? What's this?" she roared. "You're tickling me. Get off!"

"We've brought you some Goggs," yelled the Mayor. "One for each knee. We are just putting them on you. May we have our fire engine back, please?"

The people fastened the Goggs over the Knee-cap Eyes. They looked like skateboard protectors, except the front was glass, and the Eyes could blink through them.

When they were on, the Giant waded into the water to try them out.

She was delighted.

"Great! Great!" she boomed. "My eyes can see. The water can't sting them. They are telling me all about the fish they can see—Oh!—This is fun . . ."

She was in the sea for a long time, and when she came back to the shore, she said, "Here. Here is your fire engine back. I certainly don't need it now—and thank you. My Goggs are great—but,—errrr,—one thing. Could you invent some windscreen wipers for them, please—so I can wear them in the rain?"

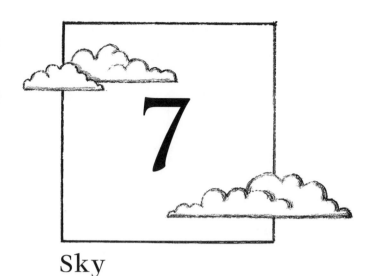

Sky

Peter Friend

"Melanie, why is the sky blue?" Linda asked her big sister.

"Not now, kid, I'm busy," said Melanie, unpacking grocery bags full of packets and tins, and stacking them in cupboards and on shelves. "Go ask Aunty Jane."

So Linda did.

"Aunty Jane, why is the sky blue?"

Aunty Jane thought for a moment.

"Because God ran out of purple paint," she said.

"I don't believe you," said Linda, and went looking for her father.

She found him in the garage, brushing dried grass off the lawn mower.

"Dad, why is the sky blue?"

"There's an anticyclone coming in from the north-west," he said. "It was on the TV weather last night, remember? It should blow the rest of this cloud away.

Maybe I'll get the lawns mowed this afternoon."

"I didn't know we had an Aunty Cyclone," said Linda.

Dad just laughed.

"Dad says the sky's blue because Aunty Cyclone's coming to visit from the north-west," she told Aunty Jane. "I don't believe him either. Really, why is the sky blue?"

Aunty Jane thought for a moment.

"Because millions of Sky People have all put their jeans out to dry at the same time," she said.

"I still don't believe you," said Linda, and went looking for her brother.

"Michael, why is the sky blue?" she asked.

"It's not blue, it's grey," he said, looking out the window. "More rain coming, I reckon. Just in time to spoil my soccer game."

"It's not all grey," said Linda. "There are some blue bits as well. See?"

But Michael didn't hear her—he was already bouncing his soccer ball down the hallway, and asking if anyone had seen his boots.

Linda went looking for Aunty Jane. She couldn't find her anywhere, but in the laundry she found Mum, fixing the washing machine again.

"Mum, why is the sky blue?" she asked.

"That's a tough one," said Mum, unscrewing a big metal thing from an even bigger blue plastic thing. "Remember Grandad's lamp—the one with all the crystal prisms? Remember how it made nice rainbow patterns on the walls? Well, the sky's sort of like a huge crystal prism, and all the other colours bounce away into space, but blue bounces down to us. Something like that, anyway."

"But why?" asked Linda.

Mum shrugged, and put a shiny little screw next to some other shiny little screws.

Linda went looking for Aunty Jane again, and found her in the back yard, sitting on the bench and drinking cocoa.

"Melanie's too busy, and Dad blames Aunty Cyclone, and Michael doesn't think the sky's blue at all, and Mum says blue is bouncier than the other colours. Aunty, really and truly, why is the sky blue?"

Aunty Jane put her finger under Linda's chin and gently lifted until all Linda could see was sky.

"Linda, why is the sky blue?" Aunty Jane asked.

Linda stared and thought, then stared and thought some more.

"Because it's really an ocean, and all the clouds are fish swimming in it," she said.

Aunty Jane smiled. "I believe you. That's a good answer. Yes, I like that one."

"I liked your answers too," said Linda.

They sat together on the bench, and watched all the clouds swimming through the sky.

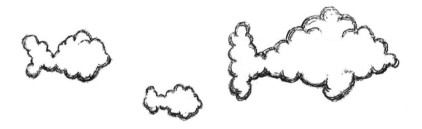

People in Glasshouses

Bronwyn Bannister

I was really pleased when Granny came to live with us. She got up early every morning and made me porridge with heaps of sugar on it. She started baking and did all the tidying up. She made my bed and never told me to pick up my stuff. She started cooking the dinner before Mum came home from work and she always made a pudding. Best of all, she told me I didn't have to eat my vegetables. You would think Mum would be pleased but instead she looked annoyed and kept glaring at Dad.

Granny was *so* cool until she moved into the glass-house—and then she was so embarrassing.

The glasshouse is at the end of our garden. There is an empty section next to our house and the fences have been knocked down so it's a clear view from the glasshouse all the way to the main road. On the other side of the house is the path. Anyone walking up our street can see the glasshouse. No one took any notice of it before, not even me. It was full of rubbish and I wasn't allowed to play inside. Now there were queues of people trying to see Granny even when she was just hanging out her washing or sweeping the floor.

The reporter from the local paper came, and said it was like a TV show. But who would want to watch a programme like *that*? The paper had a photograph of Granny outside the glasshouse, sitting on a deck chair drinking a cup of tea. It didn't look like her at all. For a start, she was drinking out of a cup and saucer when now she always uses plastic picnic mugs. For a middle, she had her hair combed differently. And for a last, they called her Mrs Hortense Williamson instead of Granny.

After the newspaper came out Mrs O'Brien from across the road started a petition. The people at number eight rang the council and complained. The postman called Granny a nutter and Mr Zabouski, who used to call in every day, began to cross the street so he didn't have to walk past our house anymore.

It's odd, I was really annoyed when Granny first moved into the glasshouse and don't get me wrong, it was still embarrassing. But I didn't like the way the neighbours were behaving. Barry Scott's mother told him my granny was indecent and Barry said that means rude.

Granny wasn't rude though. She still smiled at Mrs O'Brien and did Mr Zabouski's washing for him. She put up curtains for privacy as soon as she moved into the glasshouse. Well, she calls them curtains but really she's just hung up some big nighties and skirts on one wall and old long johns and shirts on the other. I think they belonged to Grandad. I never saw much of him, he was in hospital for years, and then he died just before Granny came to live with us. Mrs O'Brien even complained about the underwear strung up but, as Granny said, it wasn't much different from hanging things on the clothesline. It's better since I persuaded her to keep her bloomers against the back wall where they're harder to see.

Anyway, the tour buses that go to Baldwin Street, the steepest street in the world, started going up our street. I was asked to take a photo one day—Granny waving from her doorway in the background and three Japanese tourists leaning on our front fence.

Granny is very busy these days. She's always getting visitors and the post office has to deliver her letters in a van. Granny gets up especially early so she has time to bake and make my porridge. The first thing she does is clean her false teeth under the outside tap and take out her hair curlers. Once, some of her fans arrived before she was ready and Granny hates being caught in her curlers. She keeps sausages sizzling on the barbecue from breakfast time all the way to lunch. Some days it's so crowded out there, I'm surprised nobody has complained about the noise. Especially when a group of opera singers from Germany arrived. They sang so high I thought they would smash the glasshouse, and Dad muttered something about calling the council himself.

Mum and Dad have grown used to all the visitors. They have breakfast outside with everyone else. Mum and Granny make jam together and sell it to the busloads that pull up outside. Granny makes muffins and scones for them, too. She hands them out or invites people into the back yard for afternoon tea. No one is ever asked for dinner, though. That's when Granny comes inside and eats with us. Mum's back to cooking dinner but that's not too bad. She has learnt some of Granny's recipes and even does puddings.

I am still *really, really* embarrassed about the greenhouse. But Mum and Dad don't argue any more. Well, not with each other. Last week Mum had words with Mrs O'Brien about her petition and Dad shouted at the people at number eight. But this week I saw Mum and Mrs O'Brien smile at each other. And Mr Zabouski is helping Granny apply for planning permission so she can add an extension.

But the strangest thing to happen is that up and down the street and all over the town, *everyone* is getting a glasshouse!

9

How Hugo Wart Hog
Found True Happiness

Roger Hall

Hugo Wart Hog did some push-ups. Then he did sit-ups. Then he went for a trot along the banks of the river. He got home and gazed at himself in the mirror.

"No doubt about it," he thought, "that is a neat wart hog body!" Then he thought, "So why aren't the girl wart hogs crazy for me?"

But he knew the reason. He had no warts.

"It'll happen," said his mother. "One day you'll wake up and there they are. You'll be a grown-up wart hog."

"Pimples would do," he said, "at least for the time being." He ate lots of chocolate and wouldn't drink water and refused his greens.

Each morning he would peer into the mirror at his face. "Yuk!" he said. "Not a single spot."

Each day he had to walk past Max's Water Hole, where all the young girl wart hogs used to hang around. They giggled about him.

"No warts at *all*," they would say. "Just a kid wart hog."

In despair, he went to The Wart Hog Beauty Salon. He spoke to the nice young assistant. Politely he told her what the trouble was. She knew the answer.

"Here," she whispered. "Stick-on warts."

She helped place a lot of warts all over Hugo's face and body.

"There!" she said. "Look at yourself." He looked terrific.

Hugo went straight away towards Max's Water Hole. The girl wart hogs saw him coming, but didn't realise it was Hugo.

"Woweeee!" said Wilma. "Look at that cool wart hog!"

"Hey baby," shouted all the girl wart hogs. "Sling some mud with *me*!"

He refused politely but asked Wilma to accompany him to the Wart Hog Wallow on Saturday night.

"You bet," she said.

On Saturday night, he stuck on a few more warts and then collected Wilma from her swamp.

Soon they were happily squelching, wallowing and mud-throwing to the beat of Harry Wart Hog and The Trotters. Suddenly Hugo realised Wilma was staring at him.

"Your warts," she gasped. "They're . . . they're *gone*!"

And so they were.

And so was Wilma.

Hugo went home and stayed in bed for three days. Then he got up and went to the Wart Hog Beauty Salon. He went up to the assistant.

"All my warts fell off," he said.

"They do that sometimes," she said. "I'm sorry. Would you like your money back?"

"It doesn't matter," he said sadly.

"Well," she said, "I do have two tickets for the special showing tonight of the new movie, *An American Wart Hog in Space*. Would you like to come with me?"

"Oh yes please!" said Hugo. "But . . . but I have no warts."

"That doesn't matter," she said. "I'm asking you because you were polite to me the first time you came here. Today you weren't angry. You're a nice wart hog."

They went to the movie that night and when it got frightening they held trotters.

Three weeks later, when Hugo woke up, he realised he had warts all over him. Just as his mother had said.

Mother wart hogs are always right.

Mere: Ghost Investigator

C Todd Maguire

On Day One at School Camp, a picture of a ghost was waiting. It had been drawn on the dining room whiteboard.

Our teacher, Ms Brown, rubbed the ghost out, hard. She turned round and eyeballed each one of us separately. Slowly and loudly she said, "There . . . is . . . no . . . ghost . . . at . . . camp."

"Oh . . . yes . . . there . . . is," I said slowly and loudly in my head.

"Every year the first group of kids to come back from School Camp always scare the next group by saying there's a ghost," said Ms Brown. "It's a made-up story. It's not true."

"Oh, yes it is," I said in my head. How did I know? Don't ask me how, I just *knew*. The stories the kids brought back were too good. They were too real.

The kēhua had been seen. It looked like smoke. It had

48

been heard. It sounded like the wind. It had been felt. It stuck on your skin like a spider web. It played tricks while people were asleep. It took things.

That first day at School Camp, the kids made me, Mere, 'G.I.' That's 'Ghost Investigator'. My mission was to prove there was a ghost.

Night One. It was time for Ghost Duty. I was in bed, with my clothes on, in case I had to chase the ghost.

First, there was Ghost Music, whining and moaning. Where could it come from? There were no stereos at Camp, and no TVs. Second, there were Ghost Footsteps, creeping and sneaking. Third, the door squeaked open by itself.

My skin prickled. My curly hair stood up straight. I crept out of bed. I put my hands out, feeling my way in the dark. I touched a spider web. "Ugh." I pulled my hands back fast. That was no spider web. I had felt a ghost. I knew it. How could I prove it? I couldn't right now, but I would. I got back into bed and pulled the sheet over my head.

I dreamed a ghost was knocking on my door. I was having a Ghostmare. I woke up. There *was* knocking on my door. This time I'd *prove* there was a ghost. I pushed my legs out of bed. I snatched up my camera and opened the door. I ran down the corridor. I saw the kēhua walking. I took a picture but it was too dark. I found a light and turned it on. The ghost had gone.

By daylight more ghostly things happened. I got in a hot shower and it went cold. "How do you explain that?" I asked Craig.

"The hot water got used up," he said. I knew it was

the ghost. How could I prove it? I couldn't right now. But I would.

At breakfast Susana turned her back and her toast disappeared. "Hey," she shouted, "the ghost took my toast." Everyone laughed, except Susana and me. We knew it was the ghost. How did we know? Don't ask me how. We just *knew*. How could we prove it? We couldn't right now, but we would.

Austin went to his room to clean his teeth. His toothbrush was missing.

"Where is it?" asked the teacher.

"The ghost took it," said Austin.

I called a Ghost Meeting in the dining room. I had the witnesses. I didn't have the proof. I was sure the meeting would provide it. Everyone came: my class, the teacher and parent-helpers.

"Ghost Music," I read from my Ghost Report. "Heard every night. May I have a show of witnesses' hands, please?"

A parent-helper stood up, looking embarrassed. "That was my relaxation tape."

I tried again.

"Ghost Door: seen on Friday night: my door opening and shutting on its own."

A second parent-helper spoke. "Mere, I opened your door to say goodnight. I didn't hear anything. I decided you were asleep and shut the door."

There *was* a ghost. I *knew* there was. I hadn't proved it yet, but I would.

"Ghost Knocking," I read out. "On Saturday night, a ghost knocked at my door."

Li Ling looked at the floor. "I got homesick. I was looking for the teacher's door, to tell her I wanted to go home. I got the wrong door in the dark."

I gritted my teeth. Okay, I couldn't prove there was a kēhua yet, but I would.

"Ghost sighting," I read. "On Night One, a headless, legless, shape was seen floating down the corridor."

"That was me," said Singh. "I wanted to go to the toilet. It was cold. I wrapped a white sheet around me."

I worked down my Ghost Report. 'Ghost Toast' would prove it. I called out Susana's name. "Did you, or did you not have your toast eaten by the ghost while your back was turned, at breakfast on Day Two?"

"Yes," said Susana.

I grinned.

"No," said Jared. "It was me. I took it when Susana's back was turned."

I tried again. "Ghost Toothbrush. On Day Two the kēhua took a toothbrush. Right, Austin?"

Austin whispered, "Wrong. My toothbrush was at the bottom of my pack. I didn't want to clean my teeth, so I lied."

I sat, shocked. I had a list of false alarms and fibs, but no facts. My career as a Ghost Investigator was ruined.

The teacher stood up, smiling, her back to the whiteboard. "Well done, G.I. You've done a great job. On behalf of the school, thank you. Now the children will keep coming back. They were getting scared. You've proved that those incidents were *not* caused by a ghost."

Uncle Barney's Buttons

Janice Leitch

Melanie had on her smug look; I couldn't help but notice it that night when I came in to tea.

"Guess what?" she said. "I'm going to be bridesmaid at Cousin Anthea's wedding. I'm going to wear a mauve dress and get some new shoes."

"Anthea's not fussy," I replied, but Melanie wasn't listening.

"You're the page-boy," she said. "And you get to wear purple knickerbockers and a pink lace shirt."

"That'll be the day," I yelped. "I'm not going to be a page-boy. I wouldn't be seen dead in purple knickerbockers, and I'm certainly not wearing a pink lace shirt!"

"Okay, okay," giggled Melanie, "I was just having you on."

I'll have to admit though, even for a sister, Melanie looked pretty good when she put on her long dress, and they did something fancy with her hair.

My Aunty Tui tried to get Uncle Barney to go into Oamaru and get himself a new suit for the wedding.

"Not on your life," said Uncle Barney. "What a waste of money to buy a suit I'll never wear again. Besides, I need some fencing wire, and that's more urgent. No, I'll just borrow Davey's suit, it'll do me for the wedding."

We sort of wondered about this. We couldn't see how all of Uncle Barney would fit into a suit of Davey's. You see, although his friend Davey's fairly big, Uncle Barney is even bigger. Not that we blame him for being large. Aunty Tui dishes up some scrumptious meals. And she always has plenty in the tins for 'afters'.

Well, we made it to the church okay. Mum made me scrub behind my ears, but as I had long trousers on she didn't notice my knees. Cousin Anthea had asked me to be an usher, so I had the job of showing the guests where to sit.

I had practised for hours at keeping a straight face, but it was still hard not to crack up each time I asked: "Are you on the bride's side, or the groom's?" I couldn't work out whether to arm them with water pistols or laser guns. In the end Mum had to tell me to stop daydreaming and get on with my job.

Halfway through the ceremony it all started happening. We jumped when we heard the loud 'ping' of something hitting the brass flower vase beside Melanie. I could see Melanie was trying not to look at Uncle Barney, so I guessed that a button must have popped off Davey's jacket.

Then the second button pinged, and everyone in the front row was trying to smother giggles with handkerchiefs.

I sat and wondered if Uncle Barney's borrowed suit had two buttons, or three. 'Ping', yes it had had three buttons. Aunty Tui was going to have to do some mending before the suit went back to Davey. By now everyone, even the minister, was smiling. All except Uncle Barney, who was standing very still, and trying not to breathe too deeply.

After the ceremony we all had to hang about on the church steps to see Anthea and Brian come out to have their photos taken. I'd have loved to chuck confetti at them, but there was a big notice up that read: "No confetti throwing here, thank you."

Cousin Anthea wanted Aunty Tui and Uncle Barney to be in one of the photos. But when Uncle Barney took a deep breath and said "Cheese", the photographer jumped as if he had been stung. He'd been hit on the cheek by an Uncle Barney shirt button. I had to stand in front of Uncle Barney then, to hide the gap in his shirt.

There's no doubt about it, Uncle Barney's aim was pretty fantastic. The next one shot was the minister, who rubbed his ear and gave Uncle Barney a forgiving smile.

But when the driver of the bridal car had to brush a button out of his hair, Cousin Anthea went over and whispered something in Uncle Barney's ear. I don't know what it was that she said, but it made Uncle Barney smile.

He went over to his truck, and took off for goodness knows where. But knowing Uncle Barney, I had the feeling he wouldn't be away for long. I couldn't see Uncle Barney missing out on the wedding breakfast.

Uncle Barney's timing was spot on. He arrived back in the hall just as the wedding speeches were ending. We all smiled when he came into the room. It was good to see Uncle Barney back in his normal clothes again: black singlet, green shorts and big brown boots!

Āreta and the Kahawai

Patricia Grace

Terewai sat on the beach feeding her baby. It was a warm day. From where she sat, she could see the people getting pāua and kina from the rocks.

When she had finished, she sat baby Āreta on a towel and gave her a poi to play with. "You play there for a while," she said. "I'll go and help to get the pāua and kina."

While her mother was searching among the rocks, Āreta played with the poi, shaking it and banging it on the beach stones.

Not far from the shore, kahawai were swimming round and round, chasing herrings. One of the kahawai leapt up out of the water and saw Āreta laughing and playing with her poi.

"There's a beautiful baby," she said. "She's all by herself without a family. I think she's calling me."

So the kahawai swam close to shore and leapt out of

the water onto the beach. She took hold of the poi that Āreta was holding and pulled her into the sea.

Away went the kahawai, speeding through the water, pulling Āreta along until they came to the place where all the other kahawai were swimming.

The kahawai thought Āreta was beautiful. They dressed her in sea plants and asked her to dance with them. Āreta shook her poi and laughed while the kahawai circled round and round.

When Terewai looked up from putting pāua in her kete, she saw that Āreta was not sitting on the beach where she had left her. The towel was there, but Āreta had gone.

"Āreta can't crawl yet so she can't have gone anywhere," Terewai thought. "I think Titihuia and Tāmati must have taken her to play with them."

But Titihuia and Tāmati were catching herrings in a pickle bottle. Āreta wasn't with them.

"Kui Pani must have her then," she thought. But Kui Pani was just coming out of the water with her kete of pāua and kina. She didn't have Āreta.

Terewai said to Kui Pani, "Kui, I left Āreta just here sitting on the towel and now she's gone. She can't crawl yet, so she can't have gone anywhere. She can't be far away."

Terewai started walking up and down the beach looking for Āreta, and Kui Pani called all the people out of the water and told them what had happened.

The people started looking for Āreta. They looked up and down the beach. They looked among the rocks and in the water. They went back to their houses and looked in all the rooms.

They looked in the gardens and in the garages and in the cars. They looked in every place they could think of, but they didn't find her. They looked for her and cried for her for many days.

At last Kui Pani said, "I think Āreta has been stolen by the kahawai. I saw kahawai swimming in the lagoon when we were getting pāua and kina. I saw them leaping about close to shore."

The family was very sad. But the kahawai were not sad. They loved Āreta. They looked after her and took her everywhere with them. Every evening they would circle round and round while Āreta danced, twirling her poi.

By the time Āreta was ten years old, she had grown so much that when she danced, her poi would break the surface of the water.

One evening, Terewai was looking out past the lagoon when she saw something splashing in and out of the water.

"I'm sure it is Āreta's poi," she said to herself, and she called everyone to come and look.

The people came out of their houses and looked over the water. "Yes, it must be Āreta dancing with her poi," they said.

They began to wade out in the water, then to swim, but the poi was too far away.

They went out in the water with surfboards and dinghies, but it had become too dark for them to find the place where the poi was splashing. So they all went back to shore, where they stood looking out to sea and began to sing a poi song.

They sang the song louder and louder and faster and faster.

Āreta heard the singing and began twirling her poi faster and faster to keep with the beat of the song.

Soon the poi was spinning so fast that it lifted Āreta out of the water and flew her across the lagoon, landing her right on the shore with her shore family.

Her shore family welcomed her and cried over her and took her home to live with them.

Āreta was happy living with her shore family, but she missed her kahawai family.

One day when she was sitting on the beach the kahawai came leaping and splashing into the lagoon and called to her to come with them.

"Don't go with them," her shore family said. "They stole you from us when you were a baby."

"It's not really true that they stole me," Āreta said. "They thought I had no family, so they came and got me."

"Don't stay with them," the kahawai called. "They left you on the beach when you were a baby and you had no one to look after you."

"It's not really true that there was no one looking after me," Āreta said. "My mother was nearby, but there was a rock in the way and you didn't see her."

The kahawai family and the shore family began arguing with each other about who should have Āreta.

Āreta sat at the water's edge wondering what she should do. "They'll never get anywhere by arguing," she thought. "I'll just have to make up my own mind. If I stay with my shore family, I'll miss my kahawai family and my life in the sea. If I go with my kahawai family, I'll miss my shore family and my life on the land."

She thought about it for a long time, then she said to the people and the kahawai: "I want to live with both my families, so this is what I've decided to do. I'll live some of the time on shore and some of the time in the sea. During the day I'll live with my shore family. In the evening I'll go with my kahawai family and live with them until morning. I think that'll be fair."

The shore family and the kahawai family said nothing for a time. They weren't happy at first. But after a while they agreed that it was fair. So that is what happened.

During the day Āreta lived and worked and played with her shore family. In the late afternoon she went down to the sea, where her kahawai family were waiting for her to swim with them, and she stayed with them until it was morning.

13

The Opposite-Weather Boy

Chris Else

There once was a boy who had opposite weather from everyone else. Whenever it was rainy, he was bathed in sunshine. Whenever it was sunny and hot, he shivered with the cold.

The opposite-weather boy lived in a town called Blusterville. It rained a lot and the wind often blew. This was good for the opposite-weather boy because he was usually warm and calm. He especially liked the winter days when everyone else in the town wrapped themselves up in coats and scarves and gloves and the wind blew all their umbrellas inside out.

One winter, however, Blusterville had a spell of very strange weather. Instead of being stormy and wet, it was fine and dry. Day after day the sun shone. The sky was blue and there was not a breath of wind. The people of Blusterville couldn't believe their luck. They went about in their shirt-sleeves smiling and saying to each other, "What wonderful weather we're having! I can't remember the last time we had a winter like this."

Everyone was happy except the opposite-weather boy. His weather, of course, was very dark and stormy. The longer the sun shone in Blusterville, the more dark and stormy it got for him. Day after day he watched the weather report on television, hoping for a change. Day after day, the woman who read the report smiled and said, "The present spell of fine weather is expected to continue. Tomorrow it will be calm and sunny."

The opposite-weather boy's mother could see how bad it was for him. "I hope you're all right," she said. "I don't like the look of that storm you're in."

"I think it's getting worse," he told her.

"Perhaps you ought to try and get rid of it," his mother said.

By now his weather was really bad. It was not just a strong wind. It was not even a howling gale. It was a hurricane, a big mass of swirling dark cloud which blew up and down and back and forth, growing stronger and stronger from one hour to the next. He was afraid that if he did not do something the hurricane would blow him away and he would never be seen again.

"There's only one thing to do," he said. "I shall have to go to the TV station and see the people who give out the weather report. At least, they should know the kind of trouble I'm having." So he put on his coat and his gloves and his scarf and he trudged through his hurricane to the TV station.

He climbed up the steps and into the entrance hall.

The hurricane howled round his head in a roaring whirl of cloud. "Take that thing away from me!" the people yelled and they ran in all directions.

The opposite-weather boy trudged on. He went from studio to studio looking for the woman who gave the weather report. When he found her, she was just about to start her broadcast.

"Hello!" he shouted above the noise of his hurricane. "Can you hear me?"

The weather lady took one look at him and hid behind a TV camera.

"Go away!" she screamed. "Go away! You'll wreck my programme."

The opposite-weather boy turned miserably and went back outside. He stood in the street while the hurricane whirled round his head. The noise of the wind scared him. Any minute, he was sure, it would blow him away. He stared at the black and white clouds moving up and down, back and forth. They seemed to swell and roll and glow with a strange grey light. The hurricane was strong and powerful. There seemed to be nothing that could stop it.

But then, suddenly, he had a thought. If the wind was so strong, why hadn't it blown him away already? As he watched, he began to see that it would not hurt him. He gazed into the heart of his hurricane and, for the first time, he saw how wonderful it was.

When he got home, his mother asked him how he was getting on.

"Good," he told her. "I feel really great."

"What about that weather? I thought you were going to get rid of it."

"I think I'll keep it. Is that all right?"

"It's fine by me. Just don't let it mess up my sewing room, okay?"

"Don't worry. I can manage it," he said.

The Plum Tree

Paora Tibble

There's a really choice plum tree growing in our street. But just about everyone's scared of the old lady who owns it. She's always dressed in black, and she looks like a witch—that's why we used to call her Kuia Mākutu.

Every morning when we were walking to school, she'd stand at her front door and yell at us in Māori.

My friend Janey and I thought she was pōrangi. We'd run off, but some of the older kids would stay behind and get cheeky.

Her plum tree's got the fattest, juiciest plums. Us kids used to meet up in front of Kuia Mākutu's house. Then we'd take it in turns to race over to the plum tree, climb up into the branches, and pick as many plums as we could. Whoever picked the most plums was the champion.

Tame and Hinauri used to organise the game, but they never joined in. I reckon they were too mataku!

One day, it was Janey's and my turn to pick plums.

Janey was up the tree, and I was underneath, gathering up the plums as they fell.

"E Riwa," called Janey, "piki mai. I've got a pocket-knife—we can carve our names in the tree. Up there, on that branch."

I looked up to where she was pointing. None of the others had ever climbed that high. If we could carve our names on that branch, we'd be famous! I started climbing.

It was really, really high, and I didn't dare look down to see if the others were watching. Janey reached the branch first. "E Riwa," she called, "titiro mai!"

I struggled up onto the branch. There were two names carved in the bark. "'Hone and Hiria Hanson 1990'. I wonder who they were."

"Ko oku mokopuna ērā," said a voice from somewhere underneath us.

We both jumped with fright. There below us was the kuia, staring up at us. No one else was in sight—the other kids must have all run away.

"E kui," shouted Janey. "If you don't let us come down, I'll yell and yell till my parents hear me. You're not going to get us."

"He he he he he!" Her laugh sounded just like the witches I'd seen on TV. "What are your names?"

Janey's braver than me. "I'm Janey Brown," she answered. "And this is Riwa Te Kati."

"Kāti kōrua," said Kuia Mākutu. "Me mutu te mahi tāhae. Carve your names up there, next to my mokos' names. Then pick some plums for me. Those ones at the top are the sweetest."

Janey and I looked at each other. This wasn't the way an evil witch was supposed to talk. I said to Janey, "E kare, perhaps she's OK."

"Don't let her fool you," said Janey. "Once we're inside her house, she'll eat us up."

"You'd better listen to me," said the kuia, "or I'll ring your parents and tell them about your mahi tāhae. Now hurry up—I'm hungry for those plums." She cackled loudly again. "And don't worry—I won't eat you. I haven't got any teeth!"

Janey and I looked at each other and nodded. We carved our names and the year on the branch, picked some plums, and put them in our pockets. Then we climbed back down the tree.

The kuia was sitting on the porch of her house. "Is it true that your mokopuna are dead?" asked Janey.

"Yes," said the kuia. "They were about the same age as you two when they were killed with their koro. A drunk driver crashed into their car just as they were coming back from the airport." She looked at us and smiled. "When I saw you two up in that tree, it reminded me of my mokopuna and the tricks they used to get up to!"

We handed her the plums from our pockets.

"Any time you girls want some plums," she said, "just help yourselves. But not those cheeky boys. If I see them climbing my tree, I'll swallow them whole!"

Every now and then, Janey and I call in to see our friend the kuia. She makes plum jam for us to eat with our bread. We've worked out that she wears black because she's still grieving for her husband and her mokopuna, and she's lonely.

Hinauri, Tame, and the others still won't go anywhere near her. Now it's us who have all the mana round here.

Janey and me and the kuia—champions of the street!

Glossary

E kare	Hey, you
Kāti kōrua	Well then, you two
Ko oku mokopuna ērā	They were my mokopuna
te mahi tāhae	stealing
mākutu	witch
mataku	scared
mutu	stop
piki mai	climb up here
pōrangi	mad

15

What the Wind Does

Janice Marriott

We were at the bach, Mum and me and my friend Sel. The weather was the pits. Windy. Cold. The bach doesn't have TV. There was nothing to do.

We'd been jumping from the top bunk to the ground and doing mock deaths when we hit the floor. I'd scored 9, which was good.

Thud! Bone-chilling groans. Sel got a 9.1.

Then, the door opened.

"Out!" Mum shouted. "I'm sick of this."

"We haven't done anything!"

"Out, or clean the bath, both of you."

She shut the door. Bang.

"We can't go out. It's too windy," I moaned.

"Look!" said Sel.

Out the window was a horizontal world, pines and long grasses were all pointing one way, like signposts.

"Let's go," said Sel.

Outside we bent over and joined the horizontal world. On the dunes, sand stung our cheeks. We tried to look at each other but the wind tickled the corners of our eyes and made them water.

"The sand dunes are crouching lions," Sel said.

"Oh yeah?"

"The wind ripples through the marram grass, making it look like a lion's coat."

"And the lion is quivering!"

"Breathing, panting, maybe shaking with rage."

"Why?"

"Because the sea's roar is louder than his and he can't do anything about it."

We watched the glossy-coated lion. "He's going to pounce!"

We ran down to the edge of the sucking, brown sea. We yelled, but our voices were snatched away and drowned.

The sea spat foam at our feet. We ran forward, and the sea ran away from us, revealing the angry wrinkled old face of the sand. Then the sea turned and snarled waves at us, wave after wave. We ran back again.

Grey froth was left high and dry and shaking, when the sea sucked the water in again. Once dry, the froth lifted, and fluttered up the beach.

"If we had a bucket . . ." said Sel.

And there was a bucket, an old plastic paint tin, half buried in the sand. We filled it with froth.

"Have a hot chocolate."

We blew the froth at each other. A lump of my froth hit Sel in the nose. It stuck there for a microsecond till the wind wrenched it off and hurled it up the beach. We laughed and gasped and the wind and sand filled our mouths, and we coughed and spluttered.

We bent sticks and twigs and made little hoops in the sand. We batted the foam through the hoops with driftwood bats. We each got six foam balls through before we had so many rules the game became unplayable.

"A tie!"

"Tiebreaker then."

We found tumbleweeds and each of us took one down to the edge of the sea.

"One, two three go!"

We let them go and they spun across the sand.

"Go, my one!"

Mine got stuck behind a log. Sel's ran up into the pride of lions.

"And the winner is . . .!"

We tossed kelp as far as we could.

"That's not a record."

"Tis so!"

"Not. Because it's wind-assisted!"

We cracked up and ran in circles, bent double, laughing.

We found pumice.

"Hey Sel, can you hear me?"

"Sure can," he shouted into his pumice cellphone.

"What yer doing?"

"I'm at the beach."

"Me, too."

"Meet you at the top of the lion's mane."

"With a frothy hot chocolate in a mug."

"First one there's the ultimate winner."

We ran. Up the biggest sand-dune lion, over the top, down in huge slow-mo strides to the bottom of a crater between dunes. Hidden from the wind at last. We lay on our backs. A seagull was scribbling on the grey sky like a computer screen's cursor.

Then we went home.

"Start packing now," Mum said. "With this weather setting in, we might as well go home."

"What! No!"

"I just don't understand you kids at all," she said.

We shrugged. We didn't understand ourselves either. We'd been strangely different out there in the wind.

William's Words

Pat Quinn

William loved the sound of words and he liked the way they looked. But William didn't like speaking. His throat croaked, his tongue got tangled in his teeth and his words came out mumbled and mangled.

So William kept his words in a drawer.

The drawers had been thrown out when the old library was pulled down. They were long and square. They were filled with thin white cards and slid into a wooden cabinet. William had seen the cabinet at the fair. He'd stopped to stroke the smooth golden wood and slide the drawers in and out.

"Do you like that, William?" asked his father.

William nodded.

His father paid for the cabinet and helped William carry it home. William set it in a corner of the room that he shared with his brothers and sisters.

At the end of each day, William took out a card. Each

73

card was marked on one side with the name of a book, but the other side was blank. That was where William wrote his words. Then he filed the cards in alphabetical order in the long square card-file drawers.

Sometimes, if he didn't have any new words to write, he'd take out some of the old ones. He'd look at the pattern of letters, and remember the sound the word made. William found this very satisfying, and he might still be doing it, if he hadn't gone back to the fair . . .

It was held every year in the park by the school.

It had everything—biscuits and cakes, a White Elephant stall, old records and clothing and books. This time, William went to the book stall. He was running his hand along the backs of the dusty, crumpled books, his head tilted on one side to read the labels, when a book fell off the stand. William bent down and picked it up. "THE ART OF PUBLIC SPEAKING" said bold red letters on a black cover. In smaller white lettering underneath were the words: "How to Make Words Come to Life." William tried to squeeze it back into the rows of old books, but they were jammed tightly together. He laid the book across the top, but someone moved it off and it slid back into William's hand. The man behind the counter leaned forward and said with a smile, "You can have that one, William." William felt too shy to refuse so he tucked the book under his arm and wandered away to the sweet stall.

When he got home, William went to his card file. He'd heard a new word: "Butterscotch." The word looked tidy, like an army carrying flags. It made a noise like knocking on the door.

William put the book on top of the cabinet and pulled out the drawer with his 'A's and 'B's. The book slithered onto the floor. William picked it up and dusted it off. He traced the words ". . . Come to Life" with his finger, then held the book out and blew along the tops of the pages. A fine silvery dust wafted out and drifted into the open drawer. William put the book back on the cabinet. He was about to choose a card for "butterscotch" when something large brushed past his arm.

It was an albatross.

William stared.

The big bird shook itself, waddled over to William's bed, and settled into the eiderdown. It was soon joined by an ape which wound its long hairy arms around the albatross and fell asleep. More animals, an antelope and an alligator, stepped out of the drawer. Then apples, apricots and an abacus tumbled out.

William stood with his mouth open. Other words, which looked remarkably like 'abrupt', 'almost', and 'afterwards'—one that was definitely 'awful'—drifted up to the ceiling and hung in rainbow colours like a line of Monday washing. When the 'B's began—and balloons, a bantam and 'bamboozle' clattered out—William slammed the drawer shut. He knew there was a baboon in there, possibly a battle, and certainly a booby-trap of bullets.

The old book gleamed dully in a shaft of sunlight on top of the cabinet. William picked it up and opened it. The antelope butted him gently in the leg and munched on an apple. The alligator cruised under the beds, eating odd socks and old pencils.

". . . the control of words," William read, "is of great

75

importance. Words that are mumbled, swallowed, or not said at all will cause problems to their user." William glanced at his bed. The ape had woken up and was gleefully disembowelling the eiderdown. A cloud of feathers drifted up into the air and stuck to the words on the ceiling. "Words must be spoken CLEARLY and DISTINCTLY and —" William turned the page, " — PROJECTED OUTWARDS from the speaker."

William ran his tongue around his lips.

"Ape?" he whispered. The ape ate a mouthful of feathers and sneezed.

William took a deep breath. "*Ape!*" he said.

The ape ambled over to William, nibbled at the dangling word 'bamboozle', and tickled the alligator with his toe.

William faced towards the open window and repeated clearly and distinctly, "APE!"

And the ape, projected out into the late afternoon air, sailed away into the distance.

William took another deep breath and closed his eyes. "Albatross, antelope, alligator—" he went on, as clearly and distinctly as he could, "—abacus, bantam—." There was a clatter of departing hooves and claws and a whirr of beating wings. William opened his eyes to the near-normal room and added, "Abrupt, almost, afterwards, awful, and—um—bamboozle!"

The feathered garlands of words detached themselves from the ceiling and floated out of the window.

William sat on his bed and ate an apricot. Then he curled up into the soft feathers, opened his book, and glanced over the contents page. He smiled to himself.

Tomorrow he'd start the chapter called: "Making Words Work for You." He could try it on the drawer full of 'S's and 'T's. He was pretty sure there'd be a steamroller, a space shuttle, several trains, a tank, and a telescope. Not to mention speaking and talking.

But best of all, there'd be surprises and treats. And he couldn't wait to wrap his tongue around those.

Class Photo

Janice Marriott

It's my first day back at school. Everyone's being nice, which is horrible. Ben says he's going to help me catch up with the one month's worth of maths I've missed. Theo's asked me to be in his touch team at lunchtime. It's kind of yucky, but I'm coping. Until Ms Ng suddenly looks at me and says, "Henry, I've just remembered your school photo. I'll bring it back from the staff room after play."

I don't want it. I spend most of playtime in the loos. When the bell goes for class I don't move. I just sit there, on the loo, behind a locked door. I'm trying to figure out what to do. But my mind just keeps filling with pictures of what's happened.

A while back, my big bro, Aaron, was having chemo. He was usually a pain but when he got sick he was *in* pain, which wasn't quite so easy to deal with. He lost all his hair. Under his baseball cap his head was shiny as a whiteboard.

One day I came home and he wouldn't speak to me.

"What's up?" I asked.

"Nothin'," he said.

"Can I do something?"

"No," he said.

"Well quit being so down," I yelled, "cos I can't stand it!"

He pulled my hair real hard. I smacked his hand away which was easy because he was weak as. I got in trouble with Mum big time over that.

After tea, Aaron and I still weren't speaking to each other. I felt angry. And the anger made me want to do something, anything. I went into the bathroom and shaved all my hair off with Dad's razor. It's too complicated to explain why I did it. I just did it. I crammed my cap on my bleeding scalp and went to bed.

In the morning Mum's screams woke me. The cap had fallen off in the night and she'd come to tell me to get up. She'd got a fright, as you would. After we'd cried a bit, and I'd shut myself back inside myself, I crammed the cap back on and got dressed.

The cap didn't fool Aaron. I thought he'd be pissed off with me. But he grinned like a happy alien and made me show him my bald head. I peeled the cap off.

"Wooo—" he said. He was in a great mood.

Mum was smiling too. Then she said to me, "Put a better T-shirt on than that one."

"Why? This is my Hurricanes one."

"I don't care. It's your school photo day today."

"What! It can't be!" Duh! I'd forgotten. No! What was I going to do!

79

I panicked. I clawed at my head. I spun round. Then I stopped shouting because I knew Aaron was watching me. Watching me, like I was a bug under a microscope. The sort of bug he was planning to crush. "Fine," I said. "Cool. Yeah, school photo. Right."

Mum and Aaron went off to the hospital and I went into the garage.

I had this idea. OK. I know now it was mad, but at the time it seemed a good one. I painted my head with brown fence paint. Then I grabbed hold of Fungus, our old dog, and cut off a bit of hair from her tail. I sellotaped a bit of this to the inside front of my cap, so a bit of brown hair frothed out under the cap. Then I rushed back to the bathroom and dried the paint on my head with the hair dryer. It went all cracked and wrinkled, like old melon rind.

I think I was thinking that if I wore my cap—with the wisps of hair showing—I'd somehow get through the photo session.

But it wasn't to be.

They were all lined up on benches out the back of the hall for the photo when I got to school, late. Everyone stared. I'd tried to wash the paint dribbles off my neck, forehead, nose and T-shirt, but flakes of paint chips kept falling down my face and neck. Imagine painted dandruff.

Ms Ng was busy pushing girls into place on the second row, which was mixed, boys and girls. Everyone was whistling, and pulling silly ugly faces. She pointed to the front row, where there was a gap next to Theo. I sat down, fast.

Ms Ng said, "Hat, Henry," in a tired voice, and I remembered we have a no hat rule in the classroom, and for school photos.

"I, er, can't."

"Hen-ry! Take your hat off!" she roared.

Everyone stopped messing around. Everyone looked.

I slowly peeled off the cap. Some bits of Fungus' hair stuck to the cap. Some bits fluttered down my forehead. The paint was itchy as. And shedding badly.

"Hen-ry!"

Everyone laughed. The class was in an uproar. Barnaby nearly fell off the top bench he was laughing so much. Then Ms Ng's face went very white. Her eyes went all watery, but very still. She looked like she was turning into a poached egg.

"Henry, that's, er, fine. Stand on the back bench, at the end. Right, everyone. The photographer is waiting. Smile!"

No one bothered me much for the rest of the day.

That was then and this is now.

Bang! Thump!

Someone's banging on the toilet door.

"Henry! Come out."

I hang my head, run my fingers through my Number 1-type regrowth, and stay put. I know it's my mate Sam out there. I can't look at him. It's too hard.

Sam slides an envelope under the door.

"Go away," I say. He does. He's a good sort.

I look at the envelope, then I get up and open it. Inside is the class photo. In the photo I'm looking straight at the camera. There's everyone else, with huge uncontrollably wavy grins on their faces and there's me, on the end there, staring hard at the camera, proud looking, dignified.

Hey! It's cool, I think. Aaron would have liked it, too.

I go back to class and get a very low mark for maths which is good in a way. I wouldn't have liked Miss Ng being nice to me all day.

Foxy

Jane Buxton

When Nicola took her new puppet to school, she was too shy to show him to anyone. But on the way home she took him out of her bag. He was a glove puppet with big pointed ears and a smiling, foxy face. Nicola slipped him onto her hand and at once the puppet began to talk.

"Take me home right now," he said. "I'm starving hungry and I want something to eat." So Nicola hurried on her way with the puppet still talking. She was glad the puppet was a talker because she wasn't. She could never think of anything to say.

"Here's a dog on the footpath," said the puppet. "Let's stop and talk to it." Nicola was a bit afraid of dogs, but the puppet wasn't. "You're a friendly looking dog," he said cheerfully. Soon the dog's tail began to wag and Nicola felt brave enough to pat it.

"That's a good low fence for balancing on," said the puppet. "Try walking along there, Nicola." Nicola wasn't very good at balancing, but she walked along the fence without falling off once.

"Very good! Very good!" shouted the puppet, clapping its paws. "Well done, Nicola. But I'm not going to call you Nicola any more. I'm going to call you Nicky. That sounds much more friendly, doesn't it? And after all, I am your friend."

"Nicky," said Nicola to herself. "Yes I do like Nicky better." She began to skip along the footpath.

"Look, Nicky," the puppet said. "Those two girls on the footpath look as though they're waiting for you. Are they your friends?"

Nicky stopped skipping. "No. They're not my friends. They're waiting there to tease me. I think I'll cross over the road."

The puppet shook his head at her. "Oh no you won't! I want to talk to them."

As Nicky and the puppet got closer, one of the girls called out, "Nicola, Nicola! Let's grab her and tickle her!"

"Hello! Hello!" barked the puppet. "What's your name?"

"Hey! What a cute puppet!" said the other girl. "My name's Pania. What's yours?"

The puppet bowed. "My name's Foxy. Pleased to meet you, Pania. What's your friend's name?"

The first girl reached out and shook Foxy's paw.

"My name's Jody," she said. "Can I have a go with your puppet, Nicola?"

"Her name is Nicky, not Nicola!" barked the puppet. "And you can't have a go with me now because we're starving hungry and we have to go home at once."

Both the girls looked disappointed, and Pania began to stroke Foxy's long ears.

Nicky started to think that perhaps the puppet had been a bit unkind to say no.

"It's all right . . ." she began.

But Foxy interrupted her. "You can come to our place tomorrow," he said. "Come and play with me tomorrow. Do you know where we live?"

"Yes. We know. We'll come after school," said Jody. Foxy sat up on Nicky's shoulder and waved goodbye as she walked away.

Nicky's mother was in the garden. "Hello, Nicola," she said. "How was school today? I hope those girls didn't tease you again."

Foxy snapped his jaws at her. "Her name's Nicky from now on, not Nicola. And Pania and Jody are our friends. They're coming to play tomorrow."

Nicky's mother smiled and stroked Foxy's ears. "How about a glass of milk and a biscuit for each of you?" she asked.

This time it was Nicky who spoke. "Thanks, Mum. We're starving. Could you make that two biscuits each, do you think?"

And the puppet said nothing. He just smiled a Foxy smile to himself.

Takes Two

David Hill

TO: **Ministry of Science**
Parliament

Dear Ministry,

I have discovered how to invent a new pet. I take feathers or wool or fur or hair from two animals, mix them in my laboratory's secret machines, and a new pet comes out. May I have lots of money to help me do experiments?

Rhys Urch
(Slightly Mad Scientist)

TO: **Mr Rhys Urch**
Slightly Mad Scientist

Dear Mr Urch,

Here is a cheque for lots of money. Please send reports on each experiment to invent a new pet.

Rich Dood
(Man from Ministry of Science)

EXPERIMENT 1

Animals Mixed: Kitten and puppy

New Pet: Kippy

Uses: Can purr and chase sticks

Problem: Keeps wanting to go walkies. Then climbs power poles. More money needed.

EXPERIMENT 2

Animals Mixed: Rat and Duck

New Pet: Cheese Quacker

Uses: Keeps cats busy and cleans weed from fish pond

Problems: Flies through windows and steals biscuits. Much more money needed.

EXPERIMENT 3

Animals Mixed: Horse and Turtle

New Pet: Hurtle

Uses: Gives rides. Carries own stable on back

Problems: Takes an hour to go 30 metres. Lots more money needed.

EXPERIMENT 4

Animals Mixed: Parrot and Toy-Poodle Dog

New Pet: Polly Dolly

Uses: Talks to owners and curls up on sofa

87

Problems:	Yells rude words at people and chases cats. Heaps more money needed.

EXPERIMENT 5

Animals Mixed:	Budgie and Lamb
New Pet:	Cheap Bleat
Uses:	Will lay woolly eggs
Problems:	Flies up onto roof when it needs shearing. Far more money needed.

EXPERIMENT 6

Animals Mixed:	Frog and Goat
New Pet:	Froat
Uses:	Great garden ornament—something with horns going "baa-rippitt!" on a lilypad
Problems:	Froats keep butting one another. End up with lots of sore froats. Piles more money needed.

TO: **Mr Rhys Urch**
      Slightly Mad Scientist

Dear Mr Urch,

You have had so much money that we have hardly any left. We cannot help you with any more experiments. You keep having too many problems!

> **Rich Dood**
> **(Man from Ministry of Science)**

TO: **Mr Rich Dood**
Ministry of Science

Dear Mr Dood,

But my next experiment is sure to be a success! I have thought of the most brilliant mix of animals that will produce the most awesome pet with the most amazing uses and the most fantastic lack of problems. Just a teensy bit more money will do. Pretty please?

Rhys Urch
(Slightly Mad Scientist)

TO: **Mr Rhys Urch**
Seriously Slightly Mad Scientist

Dear Mr Urch,

Here is a cheque for a teensy bit more money. Please send results of your brilliant next experiment. I am pleased there will be no problems.

Rich Dood
(Man from Moneyless Ministry)

EXPERIMENT 7

Animals Mixed: Hedgehog and cat
New Pet: Prickly Purr
Uses: Will get rid of slugs and snails from garden, *and* mice and rats from house
Problems: It—

TO: **Mr Rhys Urch**
Significantly Seriously Slightly Mad
Scientist

Dear Mr Urch,

Your report on Experiment 7 arrived ripped in half. The second part is missing. The report ended just as you began describing Problems. What has happened? You said there would not be any problems!!

Rich Dood
(Man from Worried Ministry)

TO: **Mr Rich Dood**
Ministry of Science

Dear Mr Dood,

My report on Experiment 7 had to be cut short while I went to the doctor. My assistant (she is only a slightly mad scientist) posted it to you without asking me.

The experiment was a great success at first. The mixture of hedgehog and cat produced a fine new pet, with a great set of prickles, a long tail (also with prickles) and a loud purr.

But then the Prickly Purr became hungry. Instead of going after snails and slugs, it behaved just like a cat. It—and its prickles—rubbed against my legs. Then it—and its prickles—jumped up on my knees, and brushed its tail—yes, and its prickles—across my nose. This made me jerk, and tear the report in half.

So I will not be asking for any more money for new pets. But I have a brilliant idea for new plants. I am going to mix potatoes and clover to make a new grass that will turn into chips and green salad every time you mow it. I will write to you for oceans of money soon.

Oh—and there will be absolutely, totally, completely
NO PROBLEMS!!

Rhys Urch

(Your Favourite Scientist)

Mars Bar

Norman Bilbrough

On Monday, a new boy came to school. He sat at the desk next to me.

"This is Albert Mars," Mrs Janes, our teacher, said to me. "Look after him please, Jason."

He had a nose like a hosepipe and eyes so wide apart they reached his ears.

"I'll call you Mars Bar," I said.

"All right," he said through the hosepipe. He didn't look yummy like a Mars Bar.

"Why are you wearing a hat in school?" I asked.

"To keep my head warm."

He wore tight shorts like runners' shorts, and his legs were bright pink. I thought he must be cold. "Why don't you wear jeans?" I asked.

"No jeans where I come from," he said.

"Where's that?" I asked.

"Save your talk until interval, Jason," Mrs Janes said.

"Spelling test now."

I'm good at spelling. Mrs Janes gave us ten words. They were easy, except for 'wheelbarrow'. I knew I'd spelt it wrong.

"Pass your book to your neighbour," Mrs Janes said.

Mars Bar and I swapped books. All his spelling was correct, except 'wheelbarrow'!

I grabbed his thin arm at interval—my hand sizzled like I'd touched a bar heater. I jerked it away.

"You copied my spelling," I said, my hand still tingling. "How could you see it? I had it covered up!"

"I can see everything," he said. His eyes slid around to his ears. "You've got a spider on the back of your neck."

I felt a tickling on my skin. Yuk! I pulled a spider off my neck.

"I don't think Albert has any lunch," Mrs Janes said to me. "Do you mind sharing yours, Jason?"

I didn't want to share my sandwiches with a kid who sent sparks up my arm, but I said OK.

But at twelve o'clock, he disappeared. I searched the school grounds and all the classrooms. Then I noticed a blue light under the door of the storeroom. I opened the door. Mars Bar was sitting on the floor. His hat was off. An electric cord was leading from a socket in the wall to a plug in the top of his bald head, which was flashing like the light on a police car.

"Yikes!" I screeched. "What are you doing?"

He whipped the cord out and jammed his hat on. "Just having my lunch!" he said.

I shut the door fast.

That afternoon, we had singing and sports, and I kept

93

away from him. But after school, I saw him running out the gate.

"What's the big hurry?" I yelled.

"I'm late. I'll miss the ship!"

"What ship?" There was no sea where we lived. But he was racing off on his hot legs.

I couldn't catch him. I got to the corner and was just in time to see him ducking behind a row of macrocarpas. There was a noise like a giant motor mower, and a spaceship ten times bigger than my mum's car rose above the trees. There were two windows in it, just like the eyes shifting around in Mars Bar's face.

Then one of the windows opened, and a thin, pink arm stuck out and waved to me.

Wonder Waffles

Huberta Hellendoorn

"Have you had any stroopwafels lately? What! You've never heard of stroopwafels!! Incredible . . .! No, you don't *wear* a stroopwafel. You don't *ride* a stroopwafel. A stroopwafel is a waffle filled with syrup paste. Get it? Stroop is the Dutch word for syrup and wafel means waffle."

My Dutch grandmother—my Oma—has a recipe for syrup waffles in her blue recipe book.

She was born in Holland.

I like stroopwafels.

I dream of stroopwafels.

Especially my grandmother's stroopwafels.

My Oma makes stroopwafels from a special recipe book. She has saved the recipes in that book from the time she arrived in New Zealand with my Opa.

The stroopwafels are real cool, real yummy. When you take a bite for the first time, it feels as if your teeth have landed in heaven.

It takes a long time to make them but my Oma works fast. Here's how she makes them . . .

In a stainless steel bowl she quickly mixes flour with yeast and adds sugar and melted butter. She spreads a clean tea towel over the bowl and says: "We'll leave the bowl on the table in the sun. Any mixture you make with yeast needs a warm place to rise."

After an hour Oma switches on the waffle iron. She bought it in Holland.

"Nu, Sam, get the bowl with the stroopwafel mixture. I'd like you to make little balls of the dough while I mix golden syrup and butter to spread between the waffles when they are cooked."

I touch the dough, roll each little ball until it is rounder and rounder. It feels warm and soft in my hand. Oops, I drop one. It plops and spreads on the kitchen floor like an uncooked pancake.

"Never mind, schatje," my Oma says as she gives me a paper towel, "just chuck it in the rubbish bag."

Soon it's time for real action. We've made lots of little balls of dough. They look like pale marbles.

The electric waffle iron is hot and I'm allowed to put the first ball of dough on the bottom side of the iron. Oma closes the lid and presses it down, ever so gently. After a few minutes she takes the first waffle out and quickly cuts it open with a very sharp knife. She then spreads a little bit of the syrup mixture in the middle.

I stand back and watch my Oma make one stroopwafel after the other. They smell awesome! I can hardly wait to taste the first one, but I'd better wait till it's cooled unless I want my mouth to catch fire!

96

And then: WOW!

I take one bite, it tastes SO sweet and SO yummy.

I hold the golden stroopwafel in my hand, turn it around and look at it before I take another bite. It smells so good too.

My Oma says: "Sam, would you like another one?"

Do I *like* another one?

I can eat at least five more!

The Dance Hall Ghost

Diana Noonan

I used to be scared of ghosts—until one day, when I was nine, I saw a real one, and it smiled at me. It was school holidays, just after Christmas, and we were camping by a river on the edge of the dry Maniototo plains in the middle of Otago. Just before lunch Mum said to Dad, "Why don't we throw a picnic in the boot, and drive over to Saint Bathans? I'll show the kids the old hall where they used to hold dances."

So that's what we did and on the way there Mum told us about her grandad who she never knew—well, not that she can remember. "He was a soldier in the army," she said. "He and Grandma had a little farm, too—over there somewhere." She pointed out the window to the dry hills that stood at the edge of dry, grey paddocks without any sheep in them. "I used to go and stay with them there. Anyway, when I was five Grandad went to fight in a war on the other side of the world and didn't come back, and

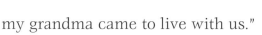

my grandma came to live with us."

No one said anything for a while after that. It was too hot to talk. Heat rose in shimmers from the road. Even the windows of the car, wound right down, didn't help. A bit later, Mum said, "There were dances—on Saturday nights in the old Saint Bathans Hall. My grandad liked to dance with me and show me off to everyone. But I don't remember that. I was too little."

Dad turned off the main road and a few dusty kilometres later we drove into Saint Bathans and parked in the shade of some poplars. We thought that we were going to die of the heat. We flopped out of the car and looked up and down the street for a swimming pool that we knew wouldn't be there. There wasn't much of anything at Saint Bathans; only a mud-brick building with double wooden doors, a post office that someone had turned into a holiday house, and the hotel across the road that Mum was heading for.

"I'll just get the hall key from the pub," she called back to us, and a few minutes later she was standing on the street again and unlocking the door of the mud-brick building. "Come on," she called from across the road. "Come and have a look."

The hall, when we were standing inside, was wonderfully cool. Light streamed through the three windows on its sunny side, making beams of dust dance as my sisters and I walked through them.

"Musty," said Mum, wrinkling her nose, and the clip-clop of her sandals echoed off the walls as she walked over the wooden floor. She stopped, and looked at a display of old photos pinned to the wall. "I wish I could remember those dances," she said.

I didn't see the piano—it must have been hidden behind one of the faded velvet curtains that hung at each side of the tiny stage. But at the same time that I looked around for Dad and couldn't see him, a slow piano tune, played with the fingers of just one hand, crept into the silence and dust of the room. Mum looked up at the stage. She began to hum softly and then, very slowly, she stretched out her arms to an invisible partner, and began to dance.

Behind me, I thought I heard one of my sisters giggle, but when I turned around to look for her, she wasn't there. Instead, in the far corner of the room, caught in a beam of light from one of the windows, a man in a khaki uniform was dancing with a little girl in a yellow dress. He leaned down towards her and, as he picked her up and swung her around, her dark hair bounced on her shoulders and she laughed. I don't know how long I stood watching them but now that the tune was coming to an end, the soldier stooped low to set the little girl back down on the floor. It was just as her feet touched the ground that he looked up at me, over the top of her head, and smiled as if he knew I'd been watching them all the time. I knew, then, what I'd known all along; that the man was my great-grandfather, and that the little girl he was dancing with was my mother.

I thought that I should tell the others but the music stopped and the ghost and the little girl disappeared into dust and sunlight. My sisters came running out from behind the curtains, then, and started dancing on the stage. "The can-can!" I heard my father call, and he began

100

playing a louder, faster tune. "Kick up your legs!" At the front of the hall my mother started clapping in time to the music. Then she began to sing, out loud, and as she did, just for an instant, I caught the sound of the little girl in the yellow dress, giggling from the back of the hall.

Cliff Minestrone

Kate De Goldi

During Foods of the World Week Room 5 had Japanese cooking demos from Setsuko's mother; Room 6 did Tongan food with Tevita's grandmother, but Ms Love's class had an Italian Chef called Minestrone.

Cliff Minestrone wore colourful striped trousers, a blue neckerchief, and a faded red apron with oil spots all over. He had long grey hair in a ponytail. He wore dark glasses and carried a walking stick. He had a small leather suitcase with knives inside and a rubber garlic peeler.

"Buon giorno!" he called to Room 8 and kissed Ms Love noisily on both cheeks. "You lika to eatta?"

"Yeah!!!!" yelled Room 8.

"Toodayee we maka the minestrone, lika my name! First you taka the onions!"

"Minestrone means vegetable soup," Freddy told his Dad that night. Dad had made soup, too. Horrible tomato with milky spots and skin floating. Freddy sipped three spoonfuls then pushed his plate away.

"Oh, I see," said Dad, "not as good as Cliff's, eh?"

On Tuesday Cliff Minestrone arrived with a large black cauldron.

"You lika da pasta?" he asked.

"Si!" yelled Room 8. Si meant Yes in Italian.

"First you taka your garleec," said Cliff. Freddy got to use the rubber garlic peeler. Carla poured the olive oil. Alex cut up the bacon and Cliff whisked the eggs and cream.

"Itsa varrry richa theesa salsa," said Cliff. Salsa meant sauce.

That night Freddy and Dad ate pasta too. Dad had pasta with mushroom sauce and grated cheese. Freddy had pasta-without-sauce-or-cheese. He poked at his lump of plain pasta.

"Your pasta is always so dry," he complained.

"What do you expect when you won't eat my sauce?" said Dad.

"I liked Cliff Minestrone's sauce," said Freddy. "It's called Spaghetti alla carbonara!" He said it just like Cliff Minestrone; he waved his fork in the air like Cliff, too.

On Wednesday Cliff Minestrone came through the door weighed down with a big bag.

"Buon giorno!" shouted Room 8. They all watched Cliff kiss Ms Love noisily.

"Toodaya," said Cliff, "todaya we do muscoli! Muscoli al forno! First taka your muscoli!" He split open the bag and fresh mussels poured into the sink with a clatter.

Freddy told Dad all about it that night as Dad was

serving up the fish for dinner. Freddy made a face at the fish.

"What's wrong with it?" said Dad. "It's from the sea—like mussels."

"It smells," said Freddy. "And it's just called *fish*. Not Fisho al forno." He waved his hands and rolled his eyes, like Cliff Minestrone.

"Is that right?" said Dad.

On Thursday Cliff came into Room 8 with six long sticks of bread.

"BUON GIORNO!" yelled Room 8. "Come stai?" That meant, "How's it going?"

"Todayee weara gonna do crostini con olive. First taka your oleeves!"

This time Billy rubbed the garlic, Kendal poured the oil and Jake and Sam W. chopped the olives. Cliff sliced the bread with his long, shiny knife.

That night Freddy and Dad had meat-loaf sandwiches with pickle and cheese. The bread was just like Cliff's but it didn't taste the same.

"I suppose Cliff Minestrone doesn't have boring old bread," said Dad.

"He *has* bread," said Freddy. "But it's not boring. It's crostini and it's crunchy and a corrverred weeth oleeves." He waved his hands and rolled his eyes and shrugged his shoulders.

"No kidding," said Dad.

On Friday there was no cooking but Room 8 ate *heaps*.

"Firsta take your bowl!" said Cliff. "Then taka your spoon!"

"Then getta your cassata," said Cliff, kissing the air noisily. Cassata was a famous Italian ice cream. And it was Cliff's all-time favourite so he had second helpings.

And then, when Cliff Minestrone had licked his last spoonful, he picked up his suitcase and walking stick; he kissed Ms Love noisily on both cheeks and called Arriverderci to Room 8. Arriverderci meant goodbye.

"Arriverderci," yelled Room 8. They waved and blew noisy kisses to Cliff as he disappeared through the door.

When Freddy arrived home that afternoon he nearly fell over with surprise. Sitting at the kitchen table with his suitcase and stick was Cliff Minestrone.

"Buon giorno," said Cliff.

"Buon giorno," said Freddy. "How come you're at my house? Where's my Dad?"

Then Cliff did the strangest thing. He took off his dark glasses and put them on the table. Then he took off his grey pony-tailed hair.

Freddy stared at the grey hair sitting on the table. It was a wig.

He looked hard at Cliff Minestrone.

"Buon giorno, Freddy," said Cliff in a very different sort of voice.

Dad's voice! Freddy felt his mouth fall open.

"Don't be mad," said Dad.

"You mean . . ." started Freddy.

"Yes," said Dad, opening the suitcase and taking out a red, oil-spotted apron.

"*You* were . . ." said Freddy. He couldn't take his eyes off Dad in Cliff's clothes.

"I was Cliff," said Dad. He took out a sharp knife.

"Every day?" Freddy asked.

"Every day," said Dad, lifting a bag of groceries up onto the bench. "Good thing, too—now I know what you really like."

Freddy looked at Dad Minestrone for a long time, trying to decide whether to be mad or not about the trick.

Finally he bent down and got the rubber garlic peeler out of the suitcase.

"First," he said to Dad, "first you taka da garleec."

24

The Whispering Mat

Kath Beattie

"I want to go home," Peleni says.

"But this is home!" his mother says. "New Zealand is our home now. We've been here for a year. This is where we live."

"Well I hate it! No one understands me."

Peleni lies face down on the mat that stretches across the living room floor.

The Konelio family brought the mat with them from Tokelau. It had been woven by Aunty Melitiana and it now covers the floor in the Konelio's New Zealand home.

When Peleni shuts his eyes he can see Aunty Meletiana weaving.

The sun is hot and the air muggy. Aunty sits in the shade humming quietly, a frangipani flower tucked behind her ear. Her fingers work fast. In and out they go.

Peleni can hear the rustle of the coconut leaves, the swish of the waves breaking on the reef. He can hear and see all these things because they've been woven into the mat, the mat he lies on, the mat that Peleni believes, tells its own story.

Peleni loves the mat with its flat wide strips of fala leaves. He loves the golden colour, the over and under pattern of the weaving, but most of all he loves the smell. A sweet dry smell that makes pictures in Peleni's head.

I want to go back to Tokelau," he says to his mother. "I hate it here. No one likes me. They call me names. 'Here comes Pelican', they say."

"Maybe that's your New Zealand nickname," his mother says.

"I'm not a bird! It's not a *real* name! I hate it."

"Maybe you could teach your friends how to pronounce your real name then," his mother says.

"You don't understand!" Peleni shouts. "Palagi don't care about my name. They don't care about me! I want to go back to Tokelau."

Peleni lies on the mat and sees the large flat island of his homeland, the warm shallow lagoon. He thinks of the patuki fish he caught there with his father. "Tokelau is my real home," he thinks. "The place I want to be."

Peleni listens again:

*Each day as the sun rises from a wide sea and climbs into the blue above, Peleni hears the drums beating. They're loud and wake everyone. "Prayer time," their beating says. "Come to lotu . . . come **now**." After lotu and breakfast, school begins early, before the sun beams too hot. Peleni sits in an open-sided room with a thatched roof. The breeze flutters through, bringing smells of the reef and the sand. He watches large crabs and spiders scuttle about as he chants his seven times*

108

table. And at playtime the other boys whisper secrets and sneak off to swim in the namo, the lagoon where they float small banana leaf boats.

"Come on, Peleni," his mother calls. "Time for lotu."

Peleni keeps his head on the mat, his eyes shut, his nose drawing in the sweet smell of Tokelau.

"I'm in Tokelau," he says. "I can't come for lotu. I can't pray or eat. I can't go to that mad school where they can't say my name and call me Pelican."

Peleni's mother puts her arms around her son. "Come now, Peleni. We're all finding it different. It's hard for us all to leave our homeland and settle in a new country. Just try and work in with things."

"Please let me go back," Peleni pleads. "I'll stay with Aunty Meletiana and go to school every day. I'll help her with the pulaka and the pigs and hens. I'll do the sweeping. I promise, cross my heart and hope to die that I'll do everything she says."

Peleni's mother and father are not sure what to do. They're homesick too. They miss their family and friends and they're tired of trying to live like the palagi and do things the way they do them. But they've tried not to let their children know how sad they are. "Let's try and make a new life here," they've said over and over again.

"Perhaps if we invite some palagi and others here maybe that will help," Peleni's mother says.

"We'll have lots to eat and have some singing and dancing," Peleni's father says.

"No one likes us," says Peleni. "No one will come! They'll say it's boring! They'll say 'Who wants to go to Pelican's house?'"

Peleni's father looks sad and hurt. "Well then, Peleni, what do you think we should do?"

"I think we should go back to Tokelau," Peleni says.

Big tears well up in Peleni's father's eyes. "Maybe you're right. Perhaps we don't belong here."

"But we've got no money to pay the fare," Peleni's mother says. "We'll have no jobs when we get there. How would we live? We'll just have to learn to live here."

Peleni puts his head down on the mat and smells and listens. He can hear his Aunty Meletiana talking, telling him about the mat and how to do the weaving, telling him the story of the fala leaves and how to prepare them for weaving. "Your mother knows these skills," Peleni hears her say. "She could teach the children. And your father knows how to make an outrigger and you . . . you know how to net fish . . ."

Peleni sits up. His eyes are shining. "I know," he says! "We'll take this mat to school and let the children touch it and smell it and sit on it. Mum! You can show them how to weave and Dad, you can tell stories from Tokelau . . ."

Peleni's dad leaps to his feet. "You're a genius, Peleni! I wonder if they know that there are no dogs there! Or that we lived in a house called a fale . . ."

"Or that we have big black birds called gogo and white birds called aki aki . . ."

"Or that a pelican is called matuku."

"You're brilliant, Peleni!"

And that is what they do. Peleni stands in front of the class and says a greeting in Tokelauan. "Malo ni, I am Peleni Konelio. You know me as Pelican, but I prefer to be called Peleni . . . or Pele. These are my parents. We have brought you a very special mat today and between us we're going to tell you a story of our first home, the place where I was born. It's called Tokelau and has three islands. The islands are small and have no hills. We lived on the main island called Fakaofo . . ."

Later the children say:

"Fantastic! Amazing!"

"Cool, eh! You come from a neat place!"

"I wish we had a mat like yours."

After that Peleni and his parents don't feel so homesick. They join in local activities and help at the school.

But on days when they're feeling sad and down, they lie on the mat and listen to it tell them about their first homeland. They hold each other and cry and say, "One day we'll go back to Tokelau. Just for a holiday, so we can see our friends and relatives. Then we'll come back to our new home and settle down again."

Three Plump Pigeons

Margaret Beames

Koro looked at the island in the middle of the lake. On it lived three plump, juicy pigeons. The very thought of them made his mouth water. He wanted them so badly he could think of nothing else.

But there was a problem. A fearsome taniwha had come swimming down the river and made its home in the lake. Now no one dared cross the water to reach the island.

Koro sighed. He did so love baked pigeon. He walked up and down the beach, thinking hard, and at last he knew what to do.

Standing by the water's edge, he began to moan and groan. "Ooh! Ow! Ouch! What a terrible pain I have in my stomach!"

When he saw a stream of shining bubbles rising to the surface, he knew the taniwha was near and he wailed louder than ever. "Oh! Poor me! I must go and lie in the hot spring beside the lake. Nothing else will make me better—but I hope the taniwha doesn't get me!"

There was a ripple and a splash. Koro grinned. The taniwha was on its way to the hot spring. As soon as it had gone, Koro dragged his canoe into the water and paddled as fast as he could to the island.

He soon knocked a fine, plump pigeon out of its tree and paddled for home. He was just in time; from the direction of the spring he could hear the roars of the disappointed taniwha.

After a day or two Koro began to think of the pigeons still on the island—tender, delicious pigeons. He simply had to get one.

Down he went to the edge of the lake. "What a feast we're going to have when my sister gets married," he sang out. "I must catch some crayfish for it." He watched for the telltale bubbles and called out louder than ever, "The best ones are by the big rock—but I must take care the taniwha doesn't get me!"

A swirl below the water and a trail of bubbles showed him that the taniwha was on its way to the big rock. Koro launched his canoe and made for the island. Soon he was on his way home with a second plump pigeon while across the lake echoed the roars of the taniwha.

For a while Koro was happy—until he started thinking about baked pigeon again. He could just taste it and there was still one left.

Back to the beach he went. He walked up and down, peering at the ground and muttering to himself. "Where can it be? I had it yesterday. I must find it."

Little waves slip-slopped on the shore and something

113

stirred up the mud on the bottom of the lake.

Koro complained more loudly. "I must find my fish hook. It's my best one. Where *can* it be? I know! I must have dropped it by the bridge. I'll go there now and dive for it. I hope that old taniwha isn't around or he'll surely eat me!"

As soon as he saw the stream of bubbles speeding towards the bridge, Koro jumped into his canoe and skimmed over the water to the island to catch the last plump pigeon. When he had it safely in his bag he returned to his canoe. He'd tricked that old taniwha again!

But—halfway across the lake, up from the depths with a rush and a roar, came the taniwha.

"Got you!" it howled. "You tricked me into going to the hot spring, but you weren't there. You tricked me into going to the big rock and you weren't there. Then you thought you'd trick me into going to the bridge, but here I am and now I shall eat you!"

The taniwha opened its mouth, ready to swallow Koro at a single gulp.

Koro was very frightened. There was no escape. He had no weapon to fight with. All he had was his paddle. Bravely he faced the monster and just as it reached him he jammed the paddle into its mouth.

How the taniwha roared and bellowed, how it crashed and thrashed. Up and down the lake it raged, but no matter what it did, nothing could shift that paddle.

Waves as big as houses smashed onto the beach. They threw Koro and his canoe up onto the shore. There he watched as the taniwha raged. The water of the lake

114

boiled, the sky turned black and great thunder clouds gathered overhead.

At last, when the day was nearly over, the taniwha was quiet. It looked at Koro sadly.

"Come here," said Koro and it came. "I'll take the paddle out of your mouth if you promise to go right away from here. Go back up the river to where you came from and never bother us again."

Slowly the taniwha nodded its huge head. So Koro broke the paddle in two. The taniwha spat out the pieces and swam away, up the river, until it disappeared into the hillside. There it lives still in its bottomless pool under the mountain.

But sometimes the taniwha remembers how Koro got the better of it and gets mad. Then steam rises from the slopes of the mountain and, if you listen very hard, you can hear angry rumblings deep inside.

26

Wet

Jane Westaway

For Sarah

Josie went to the pool every day. And every day she hated
it a bit more. It smelled of chemicals and kids' socks. It
was ear-splittingly noisy. It was slippery and slimy and
horribly wet.

She found some dry bench and sat down to wait with
Mum's bag of office clothes. A boy ran by yelling and
dripped on her foot. He leaped into the bright blue water
and made a huge splash.

Josie flicked water off her arms and legs, and checked
for Mum's head. She got a sinking feeling when she
did this—*Mum, where are you?* But there was the red
swimming cap, halfway down the fast lane. Up for air, and
down. Down for too long. Then up for air again.

Josie tried reading her book. She knew exactly what
Mum would say if she started up the arguments again.

"I can't drive back to the school for you after my swim, Josie. I work hard all day and it's something I really look forward to. It's good for me. Why don't you get in too? You never know, you might enjoy it."

Enjoy being up to my neck in cold sloppy water? Enjoy spluttering and wallowing like a big baby while everyone else darts around like a fish? Enjoy sinking?

She'd never be like Mum, Mum was a real swimmer. She'd won races and had once gone to Auckland for a big competition. That was before she met Dad and had to give it up. Now Dad was gone, and here they were, every day. Josie checked for the red cap, then had another go at her book.

On the way home, they were stuck at a traffic light. Josie was thinking about sausages for tea. But Mum turned to look at her, hands on the wheel, and said, "Josie, how long is it going to go on, you and this swimming thing?"

The sinking feeling came, but then very quickly after it, a big angry wave that made Josie say fiercely, "It's not a THING." Hating the pool was part of her, like a nose or a toe.

The lights changed. Mum said, "If you'd just give it a go."

"Don't want to," muttered Josie, staring out of the side window.

There was a silence. Josie kept still, like holding your breath and going under.

"It's ridiculous," snapped Mum, pulling into their drive. "I can understand anyone deciding they don't like swimming when they've given it a go. But not to even try

117

". . . it's feeble, it's . . . wet." She slammed the car door and marched to the house.

Josie helped with the potatoes. She stuck a fork in the sausages, laid the table, and fed the cat. And all the time, she was under water. Holding her breath. Waiting to come up for air. Waiting for Mum to give her a hug and say, sorry Josie, I was just tired and crabby.

Bedtime came. And still Josie hadn't taken a breath. She felt terribly full and empty at the same time. She wanted to cry. But that would be even wetter. She turned out the light. Some kids were scared of the dark, but it was velvety as a black cat. She let it wash over her and float her away.

She woke up suddenly. It wasn't morning because her head had a middle of the night feeling, and the light was on and Mum was standing at the end of the bed with an awful look on her face. Josie sat up blinking. Was it an earthquake? A burglar?

"Josie, I'm sorry, love . . ." It wasn't the sort of *sorry* Josie had been waiting for before she went to sleep. "Sorry to wake you up, but . . ."

Mum put her face in her hands and shuddered like Josie did when she thought of sinking into cold blue water. She said in a very small voice. "There's a weta in my bedroom."

Wetas sometimes came into the house from the bush outside. A while ago, they found one on the carpet in front of the television and Josie said it came in to watch the garden show. Mum watched her pick it up and take it outside. Mum always let her do the picking up because Josie liked wetas. They were big and handsome and shiny. They talked to you with their feelers, but most humans didn't understand feeler language.

It was weird, though, that Mum wanted Josie to get out of bed in the middle of the night to talk to a weta.

"Please, Josie," Mum was nearly crying. "Just get it out of my room, there's a love. I can't go to bed till it's gone."

Josie stared at Mum's scared face. Then she got out of bed. "It's all right, Mum. I'll get it out."

It *was* a big one. It was crouching on the windowsill, looking surprised at being indoors. Its feelers were waving messages. It definitely wanted to go outside again. Nearly as much as Mum wanted it to.

Josie walked with the weta in her cupped hands to the back door. Mum was peeping around the corner of the hall.

"Goodbye, weta." Josie knelt by a bush and carefully shook it off her hand. It waved goodbye.

Inside, her mother was sitting on the couch. "How can you?" she said, and shuddered again.

"They won't hurt you," said Josie, "not if you're gentle."

"It's how they look," said Mum. "Ugh."

"I'll get you a cup of tea," said Josie. But Mum caught her hand.

"I'm sorry, Josie. It was mean, what I said before. You're brave. It's me that's wet."

Josie let all her breath go at once. "I'm not really brave. Because I'm not scared. Like you're not scared of swimming." She thought of the weta waving its feelers and said, "What if the pool was full of wetas?"

Mum gasped.

"Do you feel stupid being scared of them?" Josie asked.

Mum nodded miserably.

"I feel stupid at the pool," said Josie. "Next time we go, I could try just putting my feet in."

Mum looked pleased and astonished.

"And next time a weta comes in, you could get a bit closer and see how interesting it is."

Mum didn't look so pleased any more.

"I wouldn't let it hurt you," said Josie. "And you wouldn't let me sink."

Mum nodded slowly. "OK. Good idea, Josie."

Josie grinned. "The weta gave it to me."

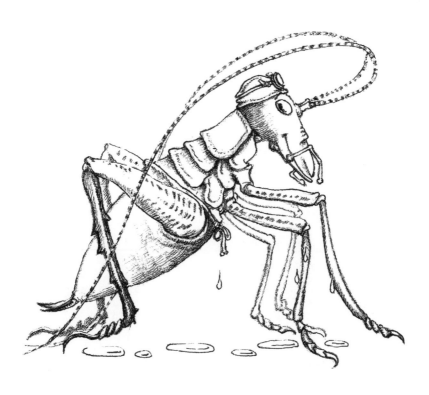

A Hāngi After All

Barbara Murison

Ani burst into the kitchen. "Mum," she said, "Mr Piper's taking us to town today to get stuff for the concert. Can I buy chicken from that new place by the post office?"

Mum put down the morning paper.

"No you can't. I wish they'd never built that takeaway. Nasty greasy stuff . . ."

"Nice try, Ani," said Rewi as he scraped up his cereal.

Mum gave Ani a hug. "Remember the hāngi after the concert tonight. You wouldn't want to spoil your appetite for that."

"Mr Piper's put piles and piles of raw meat in the freezer. *And*," Rewi said, looking at Ani, "there's a pig's head *and it's still got its eyes in it*."

"Yuk," said Ani. She kicked him under the table.

Ani and Rewi went to River Valley School, a very small rural school with only fourteen children.

As Ani and Rewi crunched over the gravel road to the

school gates they saw Mr Piper pushing an orange wheel-barrow full of shiny tinfoil parcels.

"The meat and vegies are in there," said Rewi.

"I know," said Ani. "I've been learning about hāngis too." But she turned away in case one of the parcels had the pig's head in it.

Mr Piper and Mrs Wereata, the Maori Adviser for their area, were standing beside the hāngi pit. As Ani came closer she could feel the warmth from the stones that covered the bottom of the pit. She watched as Mr Piper and Mrs Wereata put the parcels into four wire baskets and lowered them carefully onto the hot stones and covered them with sacks. A cloud of steam drifted up. Mr Piper must have been at school really early to light the fire, thought Ani as she watched him put the turf back and give the ground a big whang with a spade.

It seemed a long, long day in spite of the trip to town after morning break. Some of the kids asked Mr Piper if they could buy takeaways but he said, "You must be joking," and that was the end of that.

At last the bell went for the end of school. People started to come in the gate to the car park. Some of the boys and girls who had gone to college at the end of last year had come back especially for the hāngi. Everyone went into the community hall and sat on the fold-up wooden seats. Mr Piper welcomed them and said they had decided to turn the whole area into their marae for the evening. Some of his speech was in Māori but it was mostly in English. Mrs Wereata gave a long speech in Māori. Ani figured out she was thanking everyone for asking her to the school for the day but that was about all.

"It's time you kids understood more of your own language," said Mum.

When the speeches were finished the fourteen children from River Valley School, Mr Piper and Mrs Macintosh, who was the Teacher Aide, hongi'd with all the visitors. Then came the concert.

"It's really exciting," whispered Ani as she sat by Mum, "but I'm extra hungry now."

At half-past-five, Mr Piper said it was time to go and lift the hāngi.

Out into the frosty air rushed the families and children and all the visitors. Everyone was hungry now!

"I smell something AMAZING," said Rewi.

Out of the pits came the steaming, smoking sacks. Mr Piper lifted one of the wire baskets onto the grass and everyone picked up their paper plates.

"Would you like to be the first to taste our hāngi?" Mr Piper asked Mrs Wereata and handed her a plate with some pork and a big potato.

Mrs Wereata put some pork in her mouth and chewed in silence. Everyone watched anxiously.

"Oh dear," said Mrs Wereata. "This bit doesn't seem to be quite cooked. Shall I try another piece?"

Mr Piper and Mrs Macintosh and Mrs Wereata took some of the meat. They all chewed. Mr Piper turned very red in the face.

"Listen everyone," he said quietly. "I'm afraid the hāngi hasn't taken."

"What does he mean?" asked Ani.

Mum looked upset. "It hasn't cooked, love. They can't put it back because they've taken the sacks off and the

123

heat's gone. What a muck-up."

Mr Piper and Mrs Wereata and Mrs Macintosh came over.

"What'll we do?" they asked Mum.

"Goodness knows." Mum stared into the pit.

Although Ani felt really sorry, she felt really hungry too. But she felt good as well because out of all the parents *her* mother was being asked for advice.

"I've got an idea," Mum said at last. "Take all the food out of the pit while I go and get our van. Don't ask me any questions, but maybe we'll have our hāngi after all."

"But I'm hungry NOW, Mum," said Rewi.

"Shhhsh," said Mum. A few moments later she was driving through the school gates with all the food from the hāngi spread out on sacks in the back of the van. Everyone sat down to wait. At first it was fun to be telling jokes and singing songs in the dark. But, as time went by, they all got hungrier and hungrier and the singing and laughing died away. Then, as parents started talking about taking the little ones home for a boiled egg and some cereal for tea, lights were seen coming along the gravel road that led from town.

It was Mum.

"Where have you been?" asked Ani.

"Is it there?" asked Rewi.

Mum opened the back of the van. Into the cold night air came a wonderful, savoury, meaty, delicious hot smell.

"How did you manage?" asked Mrs Wereata as Mum started to hand out the parcels and everyone crowded around the back of the van.

124

"I went to that new takeaway place in town. You know, the one by the post office."

"*We know.*" Ani and Rewi stared at Mum.

"Well," Mum went on, "he's a nice guy that one in charge. When I told him what had happened he said we could use one of his big microwaves. Of course," she said more slowly, "I did sort of promise the school would buy some of his takeaways and stuff before the holidays but, really, I thought, it was worth it."

"Mum," said Ani. "You said takeaways were . . ."

"Your mum's really cool," said one of the college kids and Ani and Rewi went pink with pride.

Then there was a satisfied silence while everyone ate the hāngi after all.

The Moon

Adrienne Jansen

"You can't shoot down the moon," Ben said.

"Why not?" Paul said.

"Because it's stuck up there. They have a special kind of glue, and they stick it on. Even if you hit it, it wouldn't fall down."

"Yes it would. You just have to have the right kind of gun, and I've got one. So I'm going to have a go. Right now."

The boys were standing under the pine trees. It was dark, but not very dark—that sort of light-blue darkness when it's still almost light.

"Where's the gun?" Ben said.

"Here." Paul had one hand in his pocket. "You have to be very quick with this gun. You have to pull it out and fire it straight away before it gets cold. Otherwise the tiny rockets inside get stuck."

"Does it make much noise?"

"No. But you'd better stand back."

Ben grinned. "I'll just stand here behind this tree."

Paul walked into an open space between the trees. It was a new moon, a thin silver curve on a huge piece of blue glass. He said, "It's harder to hit when it's new." He stood very still, one hand in his pocket. Then there was a flash of movement, and his hand was pointing straight at the moon. There was a small 'pew pew' and a tiny rush of air.

The moon didn't move.

"I told you." Ben turned to go back to the house.

"Wait a minute," Paul said. "Look."

Ben looked. The moon gave a little jolt, then another jolt. It tipped a little, then it was hanging, by one point, from one corner of a dark empty moon-shaped socket. Suddenly it broke free and began to fall.

It fell silently, slowly turning over and over. There was a small trail of silver behind it. It came closer and closer. It didn't fall any faster, and it didn't get any bigger.

It came towards the pine trees. It caught on a small top branch, and hung for a moment. Then the wood snapped, and the moon fell slowly between the tall black branches. There was a soft thud, and it landed right at their feet.

The boys looked at it. The edge of its curve was buried in the pine needles, and there was a hissing noise, and threads of steam were coming off the white surface.

"Don't touch it," Paul whispered. "It must be hot. Look, the needles are cooling it down. Let's put more needles on it."

They threw handfuls of dark damp needles on top of the moon. The needles steamed and hissed, then finally it was quiet again.

The boys knelt down. They gently scraped back the needles. The moon lay there, cool and still. Ben ran his hand over it.

"Careful," Paul said.

"It's all right. It's not hot now. Feel it."

Paul put his hand on it. It was like thin wax with a white light just underneath it. "What shall we do with it?"

"We'll take it home." Ben lifted it with both hands. "We'll give it to Grandma. It'll cheer her up." Grandad had died not long before and Grandma was staying with them for a while.

"Watch out," Paul said. "The points are really sharp."

They walked back to the house slowly and carefully. Their feet left black prints on the damp grass. Paul said, "They look just like the place that the moon fell from."

Ben said, "We should wrap it up. There's some newspaper in the garage." He laid the moon on the bonnet of the car and the paint glowed like green glass. He folded the newspaper around the moon so that even the points were hidden.

Grandma was watching TV. Ben said, "We've got a present for you." He put the parcel on her knees.

"Well, what could this be?" Grandma unwrapped it. "Goodness me! I've never been given anything like this before." She ran her hand over the moon's surface, felt the sharp point with her thumb. Then she said, "I know what I'll do with it. Hold it for me for a minute."

She went out of the room, then came back with a long piece of cotton and a darning needle. "I'm going to put a hole here, just by the point." She pushed the needle against the surface, and suddenly the point shot through.

She threaded the cotton through the hole, knotted it tightly, then held it up. The moon swung backwards and forwards on the end of the thread.

"Now I'm going to hang it up in my bedroom." She went through to her room, pulled the curtains back and tied the thread over the curtain track. The moon hung in front of the window. It swung and spun a little, the white curve gleaming back at itself from the dark glass.

It hung there all the next day. During the day the boys could hardly see it, just a faint shadowy curve that sometimes caught the sun. But as the evening became darker, they could see it shining stronger and stronger.

The next night was very hot, and the window in Grandma's room was wide open. Suddenly there was a gust of wind. It smacked against the moon, and swung it hard on to the window frame. There was a 'ping'. The thread snapped.

The moon fell. It balanced for a moment, one curved end hooked over the window sill, then the wind caught it again, and it came free. It began to drift, out of the window, higher and higher, over the pine trees, into the blue air, higher and higher still. It never went any faster, and it never got any smaller.

The boys watched it coming nearer to the dark moon-shaped socket. There was a jolt. The moon edged backwards and forwards, as though it couldn't quite get itself in properly. It gave a last little shake. Then it was still.

"Well, we couldn't keep it for ever," Paul said.

"I've got an idea," said Ben. "Why don't you shoot it down again?"

Paul put his hand in his pocket. "I can't," he said. "I haven't got any more bullets."

Going for Gold

Sandy McKay

It's been a long day and Grandad and I have come a long way to get here. We pitch the tent and make a fire to cook sausages. After we eat we snuggle up close to the fire.

"Tell me that story again, Grandad," I say. He knows the one I mean.

"Your great-great-grandfather, George Smith was born in Dunedin in 1850," he begins. "Then, in 1861, when George was the same age as you, something amazing happened. Gold was discovered in Central Otago. People came from all over the world. Ships arrived from America, Australia and China, filled with people keen to make their fortune. George's father, Albert decided to try his luck and he agreed to let George come too. Together they planned their journey. It would take at least a week to walk there and the weather was hot and sticky. Their luggage would have to be carried on their backs. A gold pan, a tent, a woollen blanket, a frypan and some flour."

I look up at the clear night sky and try to imagine how George must have felt. How grown-up and brave he must have been to go such a long way. Imagine walking all day for a whole week!

"It was a lot harder walking than George had ever imagined," says Grandad. "In his head he moaned and groaned but on the outside he tried hard not to complain. They hiked up Mount Maungatua and down the other side again, tramping up steep gorges and rocky ledges, through bracken fern and tussock. Most of the miners walked to the gold fields but some rode horses, some travelled in wagons and some even rode bicycles."

"Where did they sleep, Grandad?"

"They took shelter where they could, sleeping in caves or pitching the tent. Sometimes they slept under the stars. At the end of the day they lit a fire, cooked some meat and boiled the billy for tea. They talked about what they would do with the money from the gold if they struck it rich.

"Gold mining turned out to be very hard work. First, you grubbed away with a pick and shovel. Then, when you had your pan full of gravel and sand, you turned it over and over with your fingers—swirling it around, then swinging the pan backwards and forwards to sweep out the rubble. After that you sifted out the black sand and what you were left with was gold.

"Young George was enjoying himself. Although there were no boys his own age to play with there was plenty for him to do. He gathered wood for the fire, peeled potatoes for dinner, and helped his father panning in the river. They lived simply and worked hard.

"At the end of the first week they had eighteen grains of gold which gave them two shillings and nine pence— enough to buy two pounds of sugar and half a pound of tea. Thirteen grains sold for two shillings which was enough to buy a piece of pork. It wasn't a fortune but it was enough to keep them going.

"Summer turned to autumn and winter was just around the corner. One morning George woke early, cooked some oatmeal for breakfast and set off with his pan down to the river. He walked upstream for a while, wading through the icy water with his trousers rolled up to his knees. He'd been panning for a few minutes when he saw it! At first he thought he was seeing things, so he rubbed his eyes and looked again. But no—there it was. The most beautiful thing he'd ever seen. He picked it out of the pan, held it in the water and rolled it around in his hand enjoying the smooth feel of it. Solid as a rock, smooth and shiny as gold! George knew this lump of gold would be worth a fortune and he couldn't wait to show his dad."

"What did his Dad say when he saw it, Grandad?"

"Albert was over the moon. He hugged George and they danced around yahooing and yelping with laughter. Albert decided to keep their good fortune a secret."

"What did they do with the nugget?"

"They buried it safely in the corner of their hut—six inches into the ground where no one else would find it. And every morning after that they walked through the icy water to the magic place where the nugget had been found. At the end of the day there were plenty of grains in the pan but never another nugget. But it was now

June—the days were getting shorter and the weather was getting colder. Soon it began to rain. It rained for six days and nights without stopping. Every creek and river flooded. The Clutha River rose ten feet in one night and the next morning George woke to see their pick and shovel floating away downstream. Albert raced after it but it was no use."

I shiver and Grandad pulls the blanket tight around my shoulders.

"They knew it was time to leave. But that night the rain turned to snow and when they woke in the morning the snow was three feet deep. Albert and George watched it piling up outside the door and the deeper it got the more they worried. They had no food left. How would they get out? How would they get home?

"And then, at last, the snow stopped. Now the frosts came. They had never seen anything like it. Everything froze. It was so cold the drips on George's nose froze. His fingers were like ice blocks.

"They got ready to leave but first they had to get the gold nugget that was buried in the ground. The ground was frozen hard like concrete and George's fingers were so cold they wouldn't work. Instead, they scraped weakly over the icy floor. Albert tried as well but nothing would work. Panic rose inside him. He knew if they didn't get out now they'd die of hunger."

"But what about the gold?"

"If they waited too long there would be more snow, more ice. If they waited any longer they might never get out.

"They were both tired and weak, there was no food

left and their fingers were numb with cold. The pick and shovel were gone and their fortune was buried six inches in the hard cold ground. They had no choice but to leave."

"What happened in the end, Grandad?"

"They managed to get out of the hut and get safely home to Dunedin."

"What about the gold?"

Grandad shakes his head. "They never recovered the gold."

"Never?"

"Never!"

The stars beam and I watch my breath fog in the Central Otago air.

"Well, Simon," says Grandad, "we better get an early night. There's a lot to do tomorrow."

He unzips our tent. Inside are our sleeping bags, some food for tomorrow, a pick and shovel and the gold pan.

Suddenly I am very sleepy. The embers of the fire are almost out. I smile to myself. Tomorrow is going to be a big day.

Tomorrow Grandad and I are going to look for gold.

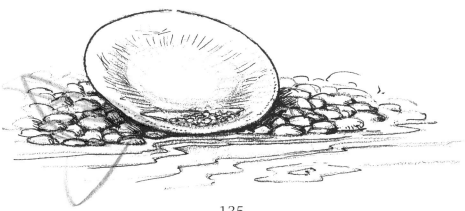

Uncle Trev, Old Tip and Old Toot

Jack Lasenby

When Old Tip lost his bark, Uncle Trev had to teach his horse, Old Toot, to bark and chase the cows up to the shed for milking. That's what he told me. Mum said it was nonsense.

One Wednesday, after she went to Women's Institute, Uncle Trev called in, and I asked how Old Toot was getting on with his barking lessons.

"He's turning out a handy horse," said Uncle Trev. "Like a handy dog? He'll head or hunt both sheep and cattle."

He held up what he was putting into the safe. "Crikey!" I said. "Where'd you get it?"

Uncle Trev put his finger to his lips. "You know how Old Tip used to run across the sheep's backs?" he asked.

"Yes."

"Old Toot can do that now. You've never seen anything like the look on a ewe's face when Old Toot's just run across her back barking."

"He'd squash them!"

"Not at the speed he moves at," said Uncle Trev. "And Old Toot isn't just the first horse to bark like a huntaway, he's an eye-horse, too."

"Like a strong-eyed dog?"

Uncle Trev nodded. "Old Toot must have a bit of Border Collie in him. It's a pity animals can't tell us their genealogies."

"But you can't cross dogs and horses!"

"When I left home this morning," said Uncle Trev, "Old Toot was down the front paddock, working my ewes into a bunch. Crouched low on his front feet, tail in the air, neck stretched out so his eyes bulged at them, his lips drawn back off his teeth in a snarl.

"The ewes had been getting cheeky with Old Tip. They knew he was losing his bark. They knew his teeth were going, too. What ewe's going to respect a dog who tries to bite and just dribbles? Fitting him out with false teeth hasn't impressed them either. Old Tip never really was an eye-dog."

"But you always said he could work sheep like an eye-dog when he wanted!"

"When he wanted," Uncle Trev nodded, "but he hasn't wanted for years. He's a sooner."

"A sooner?"

"He'd sooner lie in the shade and leave me to wave my arms and shout, 'Ho! Ho!' How do you think a man feels when his dog's hiding under the shed, and he's got to run round doing the barking himself?"

"You must feel pretty silly."

"Silly? How do you think a man feels when he's barking and shouting, 'Ho! Ho!' and he sees a car's stopped and they've got out and been taking photos of him? And all the time that Old Tip's been standing there, whistling and pretending to be working me!"

"It'll be handy, having Old Toot to help you."

"He certainly stops the traffic when he works the ewes on his own," said Uncle Trev. "It's quite a sight, a half-draught horse holding a mob of bad-tempered Corriedales just with his eye. I told you how they stamp their front feet at Old Tip to scare him?"

"Yes?"

"They only try that once on Old Toot. One bite from him, and they don't forget it in a hurry."

"Isn't Old Tip jealous?"

"Jealous isn't the word," said Uncle Trev. "He's taught himself a new bag of tricks to get my attention, but I just yawn and look away. He stands on one paw on the gatepost, with his tail in the air. That stops a few cars!"

"Do you give him a clap?" I asked.

"He's conceited enough already. That's what got him into lying in the shade in the first place, leaving me to do the barking. It's quite pathetic, actually, the way he has to take the attention away from Old Toot. He's just developed another new trick."

"What's that?"

"The old fraud gets in the creek and works the trout."

"What do you mean?"

Uncle Trev took his watch out of the pouch on his

138

belt, held it up to his ear, shook it, and looked at it. "I've got to get home for the milking." He turned the noisy little winder. "Your mother will be back soon."

"What does Old Tip do with the trout?" I asked.

"Well, Old Tip got so jealous of Old Toot, he taught himself to bark again—under water!

"He got some down the wrong way at first, but he's learned how to do it without swallowing half the creek. He's got those trout fooled.

"He's been watching the way Old Toot uses his eye. Old Tip's been getting under the water, working the trout into a bunch, and holding them with his eye."

"What for?"

"Just for fun, like a young eye-dog working the chooks round the yard," said Uncle Trev. "He runs across the backs of the trout as if they were sheep. He's watched me for years, so he should know how. He's taught himself to tickle and throw them out on the bank. He quite likes a trout for his tea, Old Tip."

"How do you cook it for him?"

"Me cook it for that old fraud?" exclaimed Uncle Trev. 'You can cook it for yourself,' that's what I told him. He puts the frying pan on. I don't mind, so long as he doesn't expect me to clean up after him. It saves me a bit in dog biscuits, too."

"Does Old Toot ever cook himself a feed?" I asked.

"Not yet," said Uncle Trev, "but the time will come. Tell your mother I put that in the safe. Hooray!"

When Mum came home, I told her how Old Toot had turned into an eye-horse, and how Old Tip had learned to bark underwater and tickle trout. She stared and said, "I warned you that you'd addle your brains if you listened to your uncle's cock and bull stories."

It's no use trying to convince Mum about what Uncle Trev's animals can do, not when she's in that mood. I sat and waited to see what she said when she found Old Tip's tooth marks on the big trout Uncle Trev had put in the safe.

Index